EXPERIENCING
the Father's Embrace through
LOSS & GRIEF

EXPERIENCING
the Father's Embrace through
LOSS & GRIEF

Finding Unbroken Courage in Times of Crisis

TRISHA FROST

DESTINY IMAGE® PUBLISHERS, INC.
P.O. Box 310, Shippensburg, PA 17257-0310
"Promoting Inspired Lives."

This book and all other Destiny Image and Destiny Image Fiction books are available at Christian bookstores and distributors worldwide.

Cover design by Eileen Rockwell

For more information on foreign distributors, call 717-532-3040.

Reach us on the Internet: www.destinyimage.com.

ISBN 13 TP: 978-0-7684-5797-1

ISBN 13 eBook: 978-0-7684-5798-8

ISBN 13 HC: 978-0-7684-5800-8

ISBN 13 LP: 978-0-7684-5799-5

For Worldwide Distribution, Printed in the U.S.A.

1 2 3 4 5 6 7 8 / 25 24 23 22 21

Dedication

I know this dedication is long but I pray that you will not skip over this. I feel when you honor those people who have honored you in life that the Father notices that with a heart of pride, so I dedicate this book to my nine grandchildren: Journey, Judah, Emma, Evie, Amari, Jayden, Jack Douglass, Ms. O... Olivia, and the boss himself Moses.

It was you—your smiles, your joy, your life, your desire to be with me—that gave this Nana the unction she needed to overcome the devastating bouts with grief and loneliness. When I think of each of you, individually or as a collective group, I never think a negative thought and my soul man is filled with life. It is because of you that I press into life with courage to live life to the fullest. It is because of you that I have learned to love life to the fullest by loving you to the utmost.

To my late husband, Jack Frost, for believing in that untapped "Niagara Falls" within me and creating a platform for me to finally believe in myself. Doing life with you was the greatest thrill ever. Thanks for ending well.

To my kids—Micah, Majesta, Doug, Sarah, Joshua, and Holly. Without your constant watch, care, and love over your mom I would have given in to the emotions of the loss of your dad and not tried to continue to carry my side of the story. Your calls and visits to check on me were lifesaving because little did you know how hard I was crying right before your call, and seeing your name on my phone caused me to remember who was left to love. You came up with creative ways to keep me feeling alive with your constant communications to me that I had value. Thank you!

I feel I must tell a couple of stories of what these guys did after Jack died to bring a little light into this story and maybe give some of you ideas to help someone else with their tragedy. I remember the first birthday I had the first year after Jack's homegoing. I was taken to my favorite restaurant by the Crews and the Micah Frosts. In the parking lot was a huge box with a bow on it. I had no clue what could possibly be inside that box. So I began to open it and Joshua and Holly who lived in California jumped out. It was the perfect way for me to celebrate the first-year anniversary of Dad's death.

Before that was the first Thanksgiving. No one knew but me, but I spent it all alone. Worst day of my life next to Dad dying. Joshua, Holly, Doug, and Sarah were all living in California. Sarah had just had Emma, and I could not get out there for Thanksgiving and her birth because she came a couple of weeks early and I had just been there for Joshua and Holly's wedding. Micah and Majesta had gone to spend the holiday with Majesta's family, so I tried to go over to my cousin's with my brother Cape and his wife Brenda. On the way I was overwhelmed with the emotion of fear, afraid of being left alone on the holidays. I literally threw up all over myself. I turned around and went home and went to bed. I swore to myself I would never spend another holiday alone. Sarah and Doug made the decision that mothers go with you over the holidays, no matter what. Their choice to do that has taken the fear out of my heart. Thank you! Children, honor your moms and dads because this is very pleasing to your Lord.

To my amazing executive board, Dave and Kris Toyne and Chip Judd, who promised Jack that they would never abandon me. They never did, and the message continues because of the hope they imparted to me to keep the message of our experience alive. To this day they are a huge part of my tribe and to others who have received their own experience with the Father's love. Had it not been for these guys and how they continued to hang out with me, you would never have received the help that you did from our message of embracing this wonderful Father. Thank you to the three of you does not adequately express my gratitude, but I am forever grateful to you.

To Bill and Beni Johnson for writing a book on courage, *Strengthen Yourself in the Lord*, and for sending me a copy after the death of Jack with a note motivating me to make choices of courage. Those choices caused me to tap into a source of unknown strength that Jack told me was within me but I could not see until I read your book.

It is because of these great examples of courage that I am able to tap into an inner strength that caused me to continue life focused on living and not allowing my loss to dictate the rest of my future.

Thank you, Bill and Beni, for your example of a life building the kingdom. First within your own family, then allowing kingdom principles that you live by to have their effect on all of the rest of us.

Lastly to my pastors who came into my life after my other losses—Howie and Terri Russell. Thank you for stepping in, helping me to navigate uncertain waters as I stepped out into a new season. I am so grateful that you provided a home for me in our church even though I could not be there as often because of my travel schedule. One of the joys of my life during this season was being able to feel that my choices mattered to you and the world and that I had value in my destiny. I loved walking in the door at the Father's House and Pastor Howie greeting me with a kiss on the forehead while saying "Welcome home" and "How was your time at so and so?" I had never had that experience with such individual awareness of me before in church life, so thank you for always being home for me and for believing in the message that we carry the way I carried it.

I also want to say thank you to some of the most important people in this project, the team at Destiny Image, for all of the hard work they have put into this. Lead by Larry Sparks and his team I say thank you. I think this was our easiest project together yet. I don't want to forget those who worked beside me to produce this and motivate me in the process. Larry, you should be proud of your team. Their graciousness when I would get somewhat testy was a true example of integrity and loyalty in the workplace. You guys rock—I mean that.

Contents

Foreword

13

Preface

19

PART 1:

The Story of My Personal Loss 25

Chapter 1:

Life in the Hood—Widowhood 27

Chapter 2:

Diagnosis or Prognosis:

Experiencing the Unexpected and Unexplainable 41

Chapter 3:

Labeled: The Ultimate Injustice 51

Chapter 4:
Which Way Did They Go?
Dealing with Abandonment and Betrayal   57

Chapter 5:
PTSD: Put That Speculation Down   67

PART 2:
Tales from the Crypt: Other Kinds of Loss   89

Chapter 6:
The Doorbell   93

Chapter 7:
The Art of Forgiveness   105

Chapter 8:
Throwaways   113

PART 3:
Survive or Thrive: The Choice Is Yours   133

Chapter 9:
A Place to Heal   135

Conclusion:
That's a Wrap   151

About Trisha Frost   167

Foreword

When Trisha asked us to write our story about processing Jack's death and the emotion of the loss and grief that we encountered in our lives, Dave's first response was, "How many volumes does she want us to fill?" The task seemed daunting and the risk of touching and exposing hidden pain felt really uncomfortable. However, our love for Trisha and her family easily trumped our hesitation.

Our story with Jack, Trisha, and the SPM team began in late 1999. We were pastors in crisis, never having been taught how to process loss and pain, and so desperate for help that on the advice from a friend we took our family to an SPM small group retreat. That in and of itself was a risky move as we had little trust for anyone, much less a guy we had never heard of named Jack Frost. To make a long story short, God met us at that retreat and we began a journey of healing and restoration *and* found a friendship with Jack and Trisha that has revolutionized our lives and ministry to this day.

We will never forget the moment Trisha called to tell us about Jack's cancer diagnosis. Our immediate reaction was that God would heal Jack and this was just another piece of his remarkable testimony. That was our thought and certainly our hope, but deep inside we had a "knowing" that our time with Jack was short and we were about to experience a loss that would rock our world and challenge our faith.

Loss and grief are challenging, and even more so because our western culture often leaves us ill-prepared to process through them. We have a memorial, we spend a few days with family and friends, and that's it. We're over it. Right? Unfortunately, that is only the beginning, but life goes on, conversations about loss are awkward, and we become "experts" at hiding our pain. We bury it beneath a myriad of emotions, and because "pain buried alive never dies" it comes back to bite us at the most unpredictable times.

After Jack died, we knew we were in trouble. Dave had lost his dad to suicide when he was a child and grew up with a mother battling cancer. Death, fear, and loss were his constant companions. I came from a broken home where violence, abuse, abandonment, and the threat of suicide were all too familiar. It seemed the only way to protect ourselves from pain was to build huge walls of self-protection. What we didn't realize was that those very walls we built to keep pain out also kept love out. Somehow, the love of God that was expressed through Jack broke through some of those walls, and we did a risky thing. We moved out of our emotional isolation, let love in, and as a result let Jack into our hearts. *You see, when we open our hearts to love, we choose to risk loss.* The problem is, when we don't know how to process that loss we tend to minimize, intellectualize, spiritualize, or anesthetize the pain. Expressing the pain of loss didn't seem to be an option, so we pushed it down and attempted to compartmentalize it to be dealt with sometime in a vague and uncertain future.

Dave was wise enough to understand that he needed help. He contacted a grief therapist who gave him some valuable tools in his journey of grief. He recounts a time when he was hurting and frustrated and said to his therapist, "I am so tired of feeling all of this. I just want it to go away. What do I have to do to fix this?"

His therapist looked at him and said, "You can't fix this. It is a part of who you are. The best you can do is *feel the pain*, process through it, and accept the fact that *you can keep living till you once again feel alive.*" He learned valuable tools in dealing with the grief, such as asking himself some important questions. What have I lost today? How do I feel about this loss today? How has this loss impacted who I am today? Acknowledging and answering these questions and allowing God's love to touch the pain was a game changer in our healing process.

When Jack died, we understood that the pain we were experiencing was small compared to what his family was feeling.

We will never forget the board meeting we had the day after Jack's funeral. None of us knew if Shiloh Place would survive or if Jack and Trisha's dream would die with Jack. We asked Trisha what she wanted to do, and her courage and commitment amazed us! She didn't want to let the ministry go. She was willing to carry the message of the Father's love in whatever capacity God provided. *Wow!* That took a level of courage that amazes us to this day. We watched her bear the grief, and instead of allowing it to paralyze her, we saw her express it, process it, and allow God to use it to minister healing to thousands. We saw her children, raw with their own pain and loss, support her and each, in their own way, continue to bring the healing message of God's love to the people around them. We saw the ministry of Shiloh Place change and flourish and grow into something we never could have imagined. That's God. When we give our pain to Him, as imperfectly as our humanity allows, He turns that pain and loss into hope and healing for others.

As we write this, 13 years after losing our friend, mentor, and spiritual father, we are filled with gratitude and appreciation for what God has done. No, we still don't understand why Jack was taken from us, but we do understand that God is always good. We know that when we give our pain and loss to Him, He heals our pain and gives us a new understanding of love and a deeper compassion for others. We understand that the pain of grief and loss changes us forever, but that change can be a positive thing. We learn that God is truly the God of all comfort, and that as we experience His comfort we can extend that comfort to others. We experience grace in a new way and it becomes easier to see people and situations through eyes of grace and forgiveness. Most of all we thank God for His healing that enabled us to open our hearts to love. That love that has changed us to the degree that we think differently, we act differently, and we respond differently. That love that had skin on in the person of Jack and Trisha Frost. That love that was demonstrated through a group of people called Shiloh Place and a love that will never fail and will live forever!

—Dave and Kris Toyne
Senior Leaders for Agape Christian Fellowship
Clearlake, Iowa

Preface

My goal for writing this book is to identify and deal with the raw emotions that are caused by loss. I hope to help anyone who is looking for answers, not just on how to live but to thrive through devastating life events without succumbing to the crisis of loss so that you can grieve healthily.

Life's experiences at times can be the best learning tools ever. In sharing the events of my life during crisis and while losing the most important person in my world, I hope to be able to help others gain a sense of purpose for this season in their life. In sharing stories of loss in other sections in this book, I hope to give the reader an understanding of how different types of loss are still loss, and if you are not careful you can stall your outcome. I hope that what I and others learned in our stories will help you to understand that the road of loss and grief can have a great ending when you make healthy choices. Understand what you are feeling and know you are safe to share your feelings, and you will end well as you walk through your life.

I personally wanted to know the *why*—the meaning of all of the emotions that I went through at that time. I had no clue how intensely I would experience many of the emotions that I have had to endure in the last 15 years. As I made choices of courage in my story, may you be motivated to choose courage for your story too.

I was determined to overcome with courage every challenge that was being thrown at me, yet I knew I had to allow grief to have its full work in me in order to thrive for the rest of my days. My problem was my motive. I was worried about how others would define me over this next season in life. I was sure I did not want to be defined as a widow. The label of *widow* caused me to feel weak or needy. I had never wanted to be addressed that way in life, so this was no different. I am not weak and I refuse to become dependent on others, including my family.

Little did I know that the greatest adventure was about to become mine. I heard tales about life at sea from Jack. I also heard the stories of his adventure in Antarctica, but I would soon discover that none of his fish stories or adventure tales would even begin to come close to living the life I was about to embark on.

I hope my journey and some of the other stories from people who have had tremendous loss will inspire you to not become paralyzed with your own personal circumstance. I hope my challenges and those in this book will help you to have the courage it takes to embrace the life that you are handed by dealing with the lies that the enemy would have you focus on. The biggest lie is that the magnitude of this loss is too painful to live with. Yes, life for me became more difficult, but not hopeless or boring because there was and is more to my story.

My good friend Rich Oliver, overseer for the River Fellowship, says, "Life is an adventure. People are a blessing. God is amazing. We're winning!"

So come with me and some of my family and friends on this amazing journey of becoming a widow or dealing with the emotions of loss and grief. I encourage you to see for yourself that life after crisis will define you, but the definition might be better than you ever thought it could be and *you do have a say in the matter.*

My goal in writing my experience with loss and finding my pathway through grief is to encourage you to never give in to any lies that would dictate to you a path that is not the destiny the Father has for you. I don't want this book to focus only on being a widow, although that could help many because 100 percent of you married couples will experience that one day. But I want to help you focus on the courage that lies within you that you have never tapped into. It will help you see yourself as an overcomer and live from that truth.

This journey that we are about to embark on should help you understand how loss can have a devastating effect upon you, your family, and others. How you deal with the emotions that you will experience over time will either catapult you into a thriving lifestyle or will stunt your destiny and even paralyze you. This will affect how you do life with others. Most of us want a healthy path with those we love and relate to. The problem is how we respond and act upon the voices we hear. The emotional health of your journey has the potential to either break you and those who love you or cause you to become healthier and more mature than before. Only you can determine and choose which path is for you.

The stories you are about to read are all true, written from my perspective or the perspective of the one who has experienced the loss. Names in these stories have not been changed to protect the innocent because no one is innocent in these stories. These are simply our encounters with grief and loss and our responses and how we came out dealing with the emotional pain of the experiences. There are many ways to experience loss. There is no one pathway of grief that works for everybody. My goal in sharing these stories is to hopefully motivate you to find the path that works for you by sharing how others found their way.

These stories are from people I know personally and am very close to. I am excited to say that, today, none of them are stuck in the pain of the loss they have endured. Every one of them not only has overcome the pain of loss and found their pathway through grief, but they are using their stories to help others who are wounded and struggling with loss.

There are all sorts of heartaches and heartbreaks in life. They say that misery loves company, and I can see how that is true. I have had loss and misery in my life, and the only company I wanted in it was to hear somebody else's story of overcoming loss—not just another story about death and the eight-stage plan to overcome grief. I have heard about the different stages of grief and they are all real-life emotions. I have gone through all the stages, but early on I had no clue what stage of grief I was in. Some say denial because I did not grieve the way most people do; some say that I was in the bargaining stage: "God, if You bless me and use me like Jack I will dedicate the rest of my life to You." Some have said I was angry and depressed, but I think I grieved Jack in many ways before he died because of the 13 months I watched him suffer every day. But for me, the reality of the loss was not just one event that happened, but loss came with many ripples. I was more prepared for the loss of Jack than I was for the loss of all those ripples that came along with the loss of Jack.

PART 1

The Story of My Personal Loss

CHAPTER 1

Life in the Hood—Widowhood

Waking up to another beautiful day caused my heart to flood with gratefulness until reality set in. Jack would not be waking up with me ever again. Embarking on the life of *widowhood* seemed to me like it was going to be anything but exciting. Living life with a legacy like Jack Frost was the most adventurous lifestyle that anyone could ever hope for. We traveled all around the world, had three beautiful children, met millions of people along the way so each day life with Jack was more exciting than the day before. Kind of like Jesus, right? Yes, as a married couple we experienced lots of trauma and situational circumstances, but I would rather have the lifetime of problems with Jack than one day without him.

Widowhood: to be empty, having no value or purpose.

This is the age of widowhood. There will be more widows in this generation than any other time in history. Why? The baby boomers are dying away.

Being a part of that generation, I thought the odds were in favor of Jack, my spouse, being the survivor. But to my chagrin, I won out, so to speak. Here I am, alive, dealing with survivorship while he is in heaven dealing with Jesus. My lament is this: Why leave me here? Jack was the better speaker, the better studier, the better intercessor, and the person everyone looked to for wisdom. He had become the father my children longed to have. So why leave me?

I know for so many the "Why me" questions really need answers so that you have the energy to focus on your next season and grieve the loss healthily. I want to encourage you to *take a season for answers, because if you don't you will become angry.*

Being a widow was not only my new lot in life but the lot of all of my children and grands at that time.

Widow, widower, widowhood—the terms even sound depressing to me. It sounds too final. It's like you are on the downward slope into eternity. Grieving was depressing enough for me, the bubbly exhorter. Even though I had experienced the loss of family before—my mom, dad, and several siblings—this loss was incomprehensible until I actually personally experienced it.

Why does the beginning of any type of change always seem to come with darkness? Creation, for those of you who are Christians in your beliefs, begins with the biblical description of the beginning of time when there was this huge, empty, bottomless inky blackness that was called earth.

*First this: God created the Heavens and Earth— all you see, all you don't see. Earth was **a soup of nothingness**, a bottomless emptiness, an inky blackness. God's Spirit brooded like a bird above the watery abyss* (Genesis 1:1 MSG).

Perfect description of how I was feeling. I remember sitting in the nothingness of life without Jack. This bottomless emptiness that I could not fix or change began to overwhelm first my days then every waking moment. The inky blackness of not feeling alive anymore. I wasn't depressed, although it sounds like I was, but I was dealing with the confusion of the chaos that now seemed to be my life.

I wanted to believe the last part of this verse—*God's Spirit brooded like a bird above the watery abyss*—because I knew that "brood" meant providing favorable conditions for my development, but at that moment I had no hope for a future. In the midst of each and every beginning, there is a condition being provided for our favorable development, even when you don't see or feel it in the moment of change and transition.

But the watery abyss surrounded me and overtook my days during this season. The abyss of loneliness had set in and left me feeling abandoned and betrayed by a so-called loving Father God. How would I live out my tomorrows? I wasn't even sure I wanted to without Jack. The hardest thing I ever did in life was not caring for Jack's needs, but was fighting the feelings of hopelessness and doubt each day while caring for this amazing legend.

In the very beginning of my story, I must tell you of a word that I received from a highly respected prophet friend of mine, Marc Dupont. Several months after Jack's homegoing, at the encouragement of some pastor friends of mine, I drove to Clayton, North Carolina to be in a meeting where Marc was speaking. I normally sit in the back of prophetic meetings simply because there are not many prophets whom I trust, and besides that, I have more words than I can ever live out, especially those promising great things in ministry with Jack. Ha, what a joke! Or was it? But I love these friends, so I came.

I sat at the back of the room hoping not to be noticed. The building was just big enough and dark enough that I thought I was hidden pretty well. Marc began to teach on the prophetic and how and why it was being reintroduced to the church and the responsibility of the church to receive it. I thought, "That will be the day!" The church I had come out of at that time would not allow the prophetic to be voiced in the church, but I listened intently because in the past I had actually believed in the prophetic voice.

Marc had gotten into the word maybe ten minutes when he stopped his whole message and said, "I can't continue until I do something." OK. I had never seen this happen in church before, so I was on the edge of my seat trying to see what was going on. All of a sudden, I heard a deep voice say, "Trisha, come up here!" I knew it was Marc's voice but it sounded like the voice of the Lord, so I obeyed instead of running out the door.

My first thought was, *I am not texting or playing on my phone, so why on earth is he bringing me up in front of the whole congregation in the middle of his sermon?* I honestly did not expect what was about to happen.

He then called my daughter and her husband up also. *Oh no—I have been given a death sentence, I am sure of it, and they are being called up to support me.* Honestly, those were the thoughts in my head, but instead I got a lot of wonderful stuff that was about to activate my new season in life. The gist of what Marc spoke over our family was this: "Father wants you to know that He is putting the adventure back into your venture."

Now what the heck did that mean? Next to my Bible, my most important study book is a dictionary. So I looked up the words *adventure* and *venture*. Adventure means elation, thrill, excitement, to incite, and to stir things up. Venture means *proceeding in spite of possible risk or danger.*

Marc, as a mouthpiece from the Father, was telling me that Father was putting the thrill and excitement back into our ministry. In spite of possible risk or danger, we as a ministry would continue to communicate the message of the Father's Love that our family had been given the responsibility to keep alive.

Up till this point I had not actually encountered the grief of the last 13 months ending with the death of Jack, the death of a vision, and at that time, for me, also the death of my identity in life. You see, my main life goal was to be content and successful in being Mrs. Ulysses Barney Frost IV. Maybe you think I should have aspired to a greater call, but I knew that moment when I said "I do" to Jack that my life was going to be probably the most adventurous life that anyone could imagine. I was happy and content to stay in that lane. So when Jack went home, it felt like my lane ran out. Confused, frightened, and yes disappointed, I was striving to find who I am without 50 percent of me.

I felt as though my value had just been stolen right out from under me, and I had no clue what direction to begin this new adventure of thrill and elation. I had ridden out the last 13 months of walking Jack through his cancer battle into the disappointing result ending with his death, so I did not feel that any other venture could match that one. Everything else would be a downhill ride from there. Fear was ever present, but so were courage and hope. The task before me was to choose a path. Either path I chose did not in any way cause me to be a failure and feel like I am loved less.

By this time, I knew I belonged and had value. Choosing to believe this motivated me forward. When the lies from others began to come, putting me into a box that they thought I should fit into, it caused uncertainty for me. These were well-meaning people who walked beside me every day, but I began to realize those same people had no clue who I was or was to become.

One person, a past employee, told my pastor and his wife I should go away. Now, what did that mean? They thought I should just give them total access to our message, allowing them to make it their own. My role could be co-founder with no voice. Needless to say, that did not appeal to me at all.

How do you allow grief to work in you without being stereotyped as a grief-stricken person who has lost all ability to live life and needs to become dependent upon family and close friends?

Also, the burden of the ministry means being dependent upon supporters to keep the ministry alive so that the message can go forward. I needed support, yet I was too proud to ask people for money or help to continue. To me it came across one of two ways. They felt obligated to us because of the help we had brought into their lives, or they felt obligated to Jack to take care of his widow. I did not want that kind of support. I wanted to prove to people that I had just as great of leadership qualities as Jack. I would prove this point to them and the ministry would be even more successful post-Jack. "You wait and see" was the motive that drove me into trying to prove something that I really was not supposed to become.

Support was cut in half within a month after Jack's death. Churches that had supported us sent me letter after letter telling us that they would no longer support the message and mission of SPM. I found out later that some of them had been asked to support only the ministries their local ordaining organizations were involved in.

Each of those losses brought disappointment after disappointment. Some of these churches and ministries we had even helped to survive, yet now it felt like they were abandoning me because I was not Jack. Did they not realize that I was a half of every story Jack told? I also was responsible for the healing that so many of them had received from our ministry, yet they forgot me. I thought the church was supposed to care for the widows and orphans above all else, especially if those widows and orphans worked as hard as I did to help others and keep the message of Father's love and Sonship alive.

I could have easily become resentful and entitled at this point had I focused on the loss more than the plan. I knew the loss, but the plan was not visible to me yet. I was new at all of this. I tried to hide my feelings by focusing on moving forward without Jack. It was only when left alone that I allowed the pain of grief to find me. I had to be strong and not allow myself to be defined as a widow because that term was a description of a weak person, an empty person. I had to make choices not to be labeled especially by those who did not know me. I remember one time when a ministry partner called me because he wanted me to come to a celebration at CBN, a very big Christian TV resort. It was arranged with all expenses paid and special seating for me. Remember, it is hard to go places by yourself, but the invite was for me alone.

Once I got there, I was escorted to my seat. Jack and I had been instrumental in this ministry, so I thought I would be on the front row with all of the guests. I was put on a row about halfway back with a bunch of white-haired men and women—older widows. They looked to me like they were all in their 70s and or 80s. I was a young widow, only 52 when Jack died. My kids were even given better seats than mine. My heart sank, thinking a terrible mistake had been made. But then I realized this was a set up by God, a defining moment for me to choose how I would be known for the rest of my life. Well, I was not going to be known for weakness or senility, which is what at that moment these white-haired people represented to me. I was put into a position that day to either embrace Marc Dupont's word over me and to live or to settle into the sedentary lifestyle of weakness and feel empty and forgotten from that day forward.

It's hard to take risks and be excited about them when you can't see the path for the fogginess of the loss. Sometimes it does take a jolt, like being put on widow's row, to help us to pursue our pathway. I want to say here that I knew from the discontentment being stirred in my heart that this was not the path for me, but I also know that my Father would have been OK and loved me the same no matter what path I would have chosen, as long as I chose to keep Him in my life.

SINGLE—AGAIN

Being a single person presents you with opportunities to socialize by taking invites at a last-minute notice. Before Jack died, socializing to me seemed more of a couple's event. Afterward, when invited by friends at the last minute to do something, I would decline because I felt kind of like a second-class citizen or third wheel. I did not like being an afterthought.

One of the definitions of *widow* is "to be empty." *Empty* means having no value or purpose. When your soul tie to the spouse you lost is not yet broken, you can become a loner and hide yourself away from any kind of social event. You see yourself as empty, half a person, and half your purpose is missing.

When I was in the throes of grief, I could bear being alone better than being an afterthought. Until you have been thrust into a place suddenly being single, you don't ever think about stuff like, "Who will I sit beside? Will anyone want to talk to me? Will I be rejected and not welcomed or invited to hang out at break times?" These are real fears, especially for a newly single person.

The first time I went somewhere after Jack's death, this actually happened to me. I went to a pastors' fellowship meeting where I had been ordained as the first woman pastor in the fellowship. I was pretty well liked by most of the people there; I did not think I would have a problem, so I chose to go. The meetings were awesome, but when we broke for lunch no one invited me to their table. I began to feel insecure. I walked over to a group of people whom I felt like I was very close to at that time, and I was asked to sit somewhere else because they wanted to be by themselves.

I almost dropped my tray and ran out of the room. Even if their conversation was a little private, knowing my situation they should have realized that I was already very uncomfortable being there by myself and invited me to sit with them. It was like being back in high school, in the little cliques that we all gathered in. Only this time I was the one being left out of the clique. This could have caused me to never want to go anywhere else where there were more couples than singles. It could have caused me to so fear going into groups that I would choose to be alone rather than trust God to place someone in my path to see me and value me enough to include me. I learned a lesson that day—as people we can never be exclusive to others. I want to be more sensitive to those around me.

CHAPTER 2

Diagnosis or Prognosis: Experiencing the Unexpected and Unexplainable

What happens when the prognosis you are hoping for is not the diagnosis that you get?

Waiting for answers has never been my strong suit if I have to wait more than a few minutes. Some of you reading this know exactly what I mean because you are just like me. It's OK, you will balance yourself out on your journey.

Jack had been coughing on a regular basis for about two months before he finally decided he should go and see a doctor. We both just thought his throat and voice were strained because of his speaking schedule. His schedule had doubled in events because of his revelation of love that he first brought home to his family before trying to convince the world. He continued to live in the experience of finally knowing that he is loved no matter what his behavior is or was. A place to feel as though we belong. Wouldn't it be out of this world if we could all experience such a feeling and never lose it?

I spend a lot of time with leaders from all over the world, and the number-one issue they all deal with is abandonment/rejection—not feeling like they have a place of unconditional love and acceptance or a person who sees their individuality unless they are becoming a bond slave to another person's ministry. Now, I am all for serving another person's vision because I learned a little saying several years ago; "You either have a vision, you adopt a vision, or you cause division." So serving is one of my finer qualities as long as I can serve/adopt another's vision within who I was created to be instead of being boxed into giftings I do not possess. Trying to serve in another's anointing is setting yourself up for failure, shame, and eventually fear of man and trying. When you feel you have to perform for another's vision to have value, you will go from one place to another looking for that place where you feel you actually belong. Many never find it, so they wander this life as what we call spiritual orphans.

When Jack Winter prayed for Jack Frost (yes, God does laugh) to receive a revelation of love that would heal his broken emotions, I never dreamed that life with Jack could be so amazingly better from then on. Our family kept waiting for the old Jack Frost, a.k.a. "Captain Bligh," to return, but he never did, no matter what happened or did not happen in a day. Jack never again allowed himself to become agitated to the point that he would be mean to me and the kids. We tried our best to agitate him to see if the old Jack and his behavior would return like we expected so we could live in the *I told you so!* But it never did. Yes, he would get upset sometimes, but when he did he would find a quiet spot and invite Father to come and embrace him. I watched him position himself to trust in a love that he had longed for all of his life and could not receive until he forgave his earthly dad for being so cruel to him, especially in his teenage years when he needed his earthly dad to be a parent to him, not a sergeant. (I don't want to rewrite *Experiencing Father's Embrace,* so when you finish this book, if you have never read our first book, the whole story is there so pick it up.)

Weeks turned into months and months into years and Jack remained the same. Loving us the way he wanted to be loved was the catalyst that motivated him to never change back into that old agitated guy.

Jack became a much sought-after speaker. He had to settle into this new person each day in his heart and heal a lot of his own personal rejection when he did not feel he performed enough to be valued in the eyes of his earthly dad, spiritual fathers, and God Himself. The key for Jack was staying in the process day by day.

I think the lasting change came from one thing— Jack was able to take ownership of and responsibility for not being a good father because he had never been a good son. He also realized in taking responsibility that he had to forgive his dad for all of the abandonment issues and for his dad's own inability to be tender in relationships, especially with his family. That story is detailed in *Experiencing Father's Embrace*. Jack tried to change so many times, especially when I would leave and take our kids. Over and over again he promised that he would be nicer, and he honestly tried. But he would fail time and time again and finally stopped trying to love us until his experience with a spiritual father who created a place for Jack to feel he belonged.

THE DIAGNOSIS

The orderly wheeled Jack back into the cubby where his daughter Sarah and I were waiting for him to return from a procedure to run a camera down his throat for a better look at what might be going on. Prior to this, the doctors had felt the worst-case scenario would be tuberculosis and the best was his vocal cords might be inflamed.

Have you ever watched a video in slow motion? This was the next ten minutes of my life as the doctor began to speak. Jack was still coming out of the effects of the anesthesia, so the doctor asked Sarah and I to walk outside of the cubby for a moment. I thought he was just being considerate, but the look on his face was very unsettling to me. I assumed it must be the worst case, TB, because they had recently had outbreaks of it in our community. He told us that Jack had adenocarcinoma of the chest cavity—a glandular cancer. They could not find a place where it had metastasized. The condition was treatable but not curable. So what did that mean? All I heard was "not curable."

The doctor began to explain the death sentence that I was listening to unknowingly. Several times the doctor had to ask me if I was OK and understood what I had just been told. I could not respond to any of his questions, and I think he began to feel as though I might need medical attention. I know now that I was in shock and traumatized. I felt so helpless—a new emotion that I had never felt before. I had always been a very strong gal and could take care of almost anything because of my upbringing and life with Jack. Jack was told that the best the doctors could give him was three months to live.

I was still in shock and everything was blurry, and I felt like I was in a tunnel hearing sounds but not able to comprehend what was being said. Again, the doctor asked me if I was alright. Of course, I was not alright; I was in shock not knowing how to process this. Finally, the message of love had become a reality in our home and we as Jack's family were able to relax in his presence and get comfortable. Jack was never going to be mean to us again, and now this. I felt like I had been through enough crisis and trauma before the revelation of love took hold. How about letting me coast in life for a while?

Jack's last message before his homegoing was on the importance of rest. I needed time to rest, but being still was so hard for me. Being still meant I had to think; I had to remember. I could not find the strength needed to take every thought captive during this time, so my thoughts when trying to rest would slide backward into the memories of the last 13 months of trying to save Jack's life.

I hate to say this, but I think for most people we learn the most valued life lessons in crisis. Life's experiences at times can be the best learning tool ever. *Life after crisis will define what you believe in, and that will become who you are.*

Crisis, the word itself, is defined as any event that is or is expected to lead to an unstable and dangerous situation affecting an individual, group, community, or whole society. Crises are deemed to be negative changes in the security, economic, political, societal, or environmental affairs, especially when they occur abruptly, with little or no warning. Like the loss of a person, job, or any major disappointment, especially in relationships. We will address that a little more in another chapter.

Oh, Jack loved to tell me I was the social light, but actually I had learned through years of living in the shadow of this amazing guy that I was quite happy with being the introvert and watching him become the extrovert. We were reverse role-playing.

At times, I hated being the one who was left behind to care for the family, the ministry, and anything else. I resented Jack having all the fun and leaving me with all the stress. He never saw the bills and the late notices. He never was there when the kids needed a doctor and I had to pray through until they were healed because we had no money to take them to the doctor. He was never there for the crucial moments, the crisis moments, or most of the fun moments. He was the absentee dad and I had become General Mom. (See our CD on father/mother types.)

"Who is this person I have become? I don't know her anymore." Resentment continued to build in my heart; my life with Jack would never be fulfilling for anyone but him. I remember my world being so full of the stress and worry of making sure everything went smoothly that I sat outside in front of our own house and cried out to God, "Why does one of us have to die so the other one can live?"

In the next few weeks, a second opinion was given to us and indeed it was the cancer that we feared. "We can make your husband comfortable, but he will die in three to six months." The longest contender of the battle with adeno carcinoma only lived six months. Instinctively, my flesh man went to blame shifting and the whole *what if* game was beginning its first round of play. *Treatable but not curable*—those words continued to haunt me as we spent the next 13 months going from clinic to clinic trying to find our cure. Unfortunately, our prognosis would not turn into the path we had hoped for.

Jack went to be with Jesus almost exactly 13 months later. But his death was not the end of the story. His example of embracing the love that was introduced to him by Jack Winter has caused so many people to find their healing and to give it first to their families. Thirteen years later, our family legacy and the legend of Jack Frost is still changing lives and healing hearts by helping seeking people find their story, redeem the damage, and begin to move forward. I hope this is you!

CHAPTER 3

Labeled: The Ultimate Injustice

As members of the human race, there are times when humans act very inhumane. People label you according to who they think you are instead of finding out who you really are. It takes a lot of energy out of you to constantly be fighting the invisible force of another's label on you. *Label* means to assign to a category, especially inaccurately or restrictively.

Being married to one of the most adventurous people on earth and now living life without him caused me to experience great levels of loneliness. I had become used to a life of loneliness when Jack was gone working, but I knew he would always return. We lived life together, we did ministry together, we wrote books together. We were together the majority of our days when Jack was in town. I remember one time Jack and I were going through ministry for something totally different and the prayer counselor Mark Sandford looked right at me and said, "Everything you are dealing with at this moment is wired to loneliness." It hit me so hard I began to cry the ugly cry. And Jack was still alive! Yet Mark said, "Trisha, you are the loneliest person I have ever met." I learned that day that loneliness will never go away until you deal with the unmet needs you have. I learned to stop fearing that sharing my needs would make me look weak and unattractive to Jack because he needed a strong person living life with him.

I was surrounded by friends and at that time two of my kids were still at home, yet I had to admit Mark was right. There had to be a reason to make a better plan for the rest of our life. It was not fair that Jack was the only one getting to enjoy life.

Fear, especially the fear of man, is probably one of the hardest emotions to change. It shows up everywhere in almost everything you do. So we made a plan to build a retirement home on the water and have boats and skis and big bedrooms for each child's family when they were home. Life growing up for our kids was filled with adventurous vacations. I think they each would tell you our summer lake house vacations were the best ones (thank you Mike and Patty Hardegree). So much laughter and joy and family time. So Jack and I took our inheritance and bought a piece of property on the inland waterway and began to move forward on building a play house for us and our kids and their kids.

Unfortunately, in the midst of the fun of the plan, we got the news that Jack had cancer. Now our dilemma was to sell or not sell the property. In the uncertainty of life, should we build our dream house or not? If Jack died, then would I be able to afford this new home? Some of our financial friends who were not placing a death label on Jack but who were concerned for our future began to offer much-needed advice, making sure that we would be OK no matter what turnout we faced.

Earlier in life I had been labeled "Little Miss Much Afraid," and I had not received total healing from that label, even though Jack was now living in his revelation of how much he was loved exampling this to his family. *Tough decisions during crisis will cause you to have to evaluate not only what it is you believe but what you are able to live, and that is what you will be known for the rest of your life. We decided to live our life as if we were living, not dying.*

Neither Jack nor I wanted to be labeled as "leaders without courage." We did not want to live out our lives in fear and uncertainty. In the midst of your life crisis or circumstance, my advice to you would be the same.

But Jack did die.

He did, however, get to live in our beautiful play house for six weeks, and the building of that home brought life into Jack's days. Sometimes having something to hope for can be a wonderful distraction from the pain we might be enduring during the process. I know it was for Jack.

I lived there for 13 years after Jack's death. I called the house the Resting Place, the House that Jack Built. Never one day have I regretted the decision to live life as though we were living and not dying, because when you choose life you position yourself into a win-win situation. Even though my story did not turn out like I hoped for, life was still good and Jack would have been so thrilled that I got to live in this safe haven of a home, sharing it with world and local leaders as they too needed a place to land for a season of rest. I needed a haven to be still and listen for what's next.

Attacks continued against the "Father loves you" message, and I continued being the brunt of labels from people who did not know me during this season. The only reason those labels stuck for any length of time was I chose to believe them myself, so those labels became self-inflicting wounds. Those people did not know me or who I am, but evidently neither did I. I did not know the person I had become, even though I had made my own choices to live life and to be known for loving others at all costs.

That choice is a choice that had a price tag that I and my family have paid by keeping the message alive. I have been labeled a widow; a weak, empty person; and a failure by those who thought I could not lead. They could not in a million years have embraced that I was God's choice for that moment because they were looking at my past weaknesses and not the woman of courage I embraced. I believed those who inspired me through their encouragement, knowing what He knows about me.

In my time of need, I felt abandoned but somehow got the courage to move forward. I want to thank Marc Dupont for being brave enough to label me as adventurous. I want to thank Bill and Beni Johnson again for calling me courageous, because in listening to what I was yet to become I was able to look within to see what Father had created in me. You can too by embracing the truth that there is a plan for your life that involves some pain, yes, but it also involves the completion of a journey that you get the thrill to live. I chose to live in the adventure of the venture, with thrill and excitement, yet there was the possibility of risk and danger.

Which Way Did They Go?

Dealing with Abandonment and Betrayal

It is not just hard for the person who is going through a loss, but it is also very hard for others to know how to help them along in their path of grieving healthily, especially when you have your own life to live.

After the death of Jack, some of the things people said to me and my kids were kind, and some were not so kind. I will discuss that more in the last chapter. But in this chapter, I want to tell the story of the greatest betrayal of my life. When devastation happens in your life, how you overcome it will either make you bitter or better. I need to tell this story because I am better and not bitter. This story is told from my perspective. I was not sure whether to tell this story, so I asked Jack's best friend, Chip Judd, and he gave me wonderful advice: "It happened. Just tell it from your perspective, letting the reader know this is your perspective of the loss." So here goes.

It is hard to receive help from others who can't possibly understand your trauma, especially if you have never lost much in your life. This is not only applicable for someone who has lost a loved one, but can be applicable for any type of loss.

I deal with people daily who have lost jobs, relationships, value, credibility, church homes, normal homes, etc. Loss is loss no matter what form it comes in for you. When we hide the effects of grief in our lives, we become paralyzed and live life in survival mode, just barely getting by.

So many people were speaking or trying to speak into my life in my situation, but I could not hear any of them. I had a pile of books or brochures or pamphlets or printed-out words that stacked almost two feet high, and I left them in the corner because every time I tried to pick something up it was like I went blind. Everything was a blur; I simply could not focus.

Well-meaning people tried to tell me I was in a depression. I had been friends with depression in the past, so I knew that was not the case. It was simply too soon to make a plan for the rest of my life, so I took some time off and let the staff we had left run things until I could return.

During this time of leave, I kept asking Father what He wanted from me for the rest of my life. I like to ask God, "What is it You're doing in the world and what is my role?" I think people get into trouble when they try to fulfill a role that is not theirs to live. I love the saying, "If you is who you ain't then you ain't who you is." What wonderful advice! I was listening to voices telling me who I wasn't. Trying to please those voices I became who I ain't so who I is was missing.

It was during this season that confusion set into my life. Some people knew exactly what I was supposed to be about. Some people did not know what to say or pray so they said or did nothing. Then there were those like my friend and board member Kris Toyne who asked me one simple question: "What do you want to do with the rest of your life and the life of the ministry?" I was looking for someone else to tell me, not realizing that I had to confront that hard decision for myself. Being faced with the reality that it truly was my decision to make, clarity came.

You often hear that you should never make any major life decisions until one year has passed from the tragedy, but in my case this was not the ideal way to move forward. There was an international ministry that was in the prime of its life when tragedy struck, loss happened, and confusion tried to dictate the outcome. I had to step in and make some hard choices, but thank God I had an amazing board in Chip Judd and Dave and Kris Toyne. I did not have to walk the path by myself, but I did have to make the choice of what to do with the ministry, knowing they would support any decision I made.

Still, the fear of "what if" made a home in my mind and heart and slowed down the process of moving forward. I was so scared that my board and family would be disappointed in me. This fear caused me to begin to embrace the lies and rumors that were already starting to stir that I would do it all wrong and the ministry would die. Thank God for board members who would not allow me to think like that.

I want to encourage you that you too have the authority to choose in your loss and trauma. I am saying to you what Bill Johnson said to me during this season: "I pray you make the choice of courage" (see Josh. 1:9).

During this time of waiting for the Lord to drop a plan in my lap in a thunderous, climatic kind of way, I was told about what people were saying about my capabilities. "She is not Jack, she will run the ministry into the ground, it's a 'Father loves you' ministry so she should turn it over to a guy." One person said I had mental disorders because of Jack's death. Now, if you know me at all, the mental disorders were there before Jack died!

The greatest verbal attacks against me came during the time of trying to figure life out. I was told I just needed to go away. Just go be a grandmother and let another take over the ministry. There was more said, but let's look at this for a moment. I honestly considered this as an option until I learned the source of the statement was a person trying to shut my voice down. It was a close person God had used in my life many times before. Betrayal is hard no matter who the betrayer is. King David also was betrayed by his counselor and friend. His response was that he might have handled it better had it come from a stranger, but when betrayal and abandonment come from a trusted source it is harder to let go so your wound can heal and your soul be cleansed.

I choose to believe their motives were well-intended, but it was very difficult to believe that they were for me. Other people were pulled in, and I was getting mixed messages from voices I would have trusted without hesitation in the past. When I did not feel that this was good counsel, they removed me from their life. The loss of a friend and spiritual mentor was almost as hard as losing Jack.

One thing I learned from this was you should never allow someone that much control over your decisions. Always listen to wise counsel, but be OK saying no to any counsel you feel is against God's will for your life.

It is so important to hear the voice of God before man. Even in the midst of loss, you never lose the ability to hear from Him if you are listening. I began to listen to Him first, so my identity changed. When your identity changes, people who don't know who you really are have no clue what to do with this new person. It's not that I rebelled against their wisdom; they were trying to fit me into a box that was not big enough for this next season. So little by little, they began to distance themselves even more from me.

When people don't feel like they can control you, they will either discredit you or alienate you. I experienced abandonment from them and from others. At this time, their influence was greater than mine, so people listened to what they said. Some even called me a *Christian feminist/liberalist* because I spoke on the mother heart of Father God. I remember the day that I received my first phone call calling me this, and I asked them why they drew that conclusion about me. They had no answer because they had not even listened to one teaching by me or read any of my notes on the topic of the mother's heart. When they called me that name I admit I actually got very defensive and responded wrongly, so they abruptly ended the phone call with the ultimatum that this message would never be spoken in their church and if I wanted to continue our friendship I needed to listen to them because they had my best interests at heart. I believe that this person really did, but I also knew that Father had given me the mandate to keep our message alive, and this was a huge part of it.

In my point of view, I had to prove to people that I could keep the ministry alive as well as Jack had. "I will show them." I made the decision to take over the ministry, because in our bylaws I was Jack's choice to replace him. I really did not believe I could do it either, but now I had a reason—but a wrong motive—to go on. I would prove how wrong these people were about me.

Motives can hinder everything you do or can promote you into your position in life. I actually did want to become the person Jack saw in me when he called me a force like Niagara Falls (good motive) but I went about it with vengeance (wrong motive).

So I made choices to forgive those who did not know me, to forgive those who forgot me, to forgive myself for bad choices I made in moving forward, to ask those I hurt to forgive me, and finally to forgive Father God. And I did move forward with leading Shiloh Place Ministries. With the blessing of those who knew me and the separation and abandonment of those who did not, I began to travel, do counseling, and write books. I carried the message of how much you are loved by a Father who is actually God and has a path for your journey. Wrong motive or not, the message needed to continue, and Father would balance me out. I believe that is the result of every act of obedience. Even when you don't know where you are headed, just get started. Submit to Him and His voice, and I promise you, you will succeed. I succeeded even when I did not feel like I was making forward motion. Two steps forward, one step back—if you actually do that, you will see that you are still making forward motion.

Someone once told me not to bite off more than I could chew. I told them I'd rather choke on greatness than nibble on mediocrity.

—Author unknown

With the above statement as my direction and motto for the rest of my life, I finally knew where I was headed and my role in life in His plan for me. I knew my identity now! How did I figure it out? I began listening more to the voices of life and refused to stay stuck in the pain of rejection and abandonment from the voices who did not know me.

Loss can destabilize your destiny if you allow bitterness and unforgiveness to overpower your emotions. Grief for the loss needs to happen, so I encourage you to find your path for grief by confronting the voices that might keep you focused on the loss more than your identity for the future. Focus on who you are instead of who you are not. As you read on, you are going to hear actual testimonies of people who have made some amazing choices of courage to confront loss by finding and walking their path of grief with Him and ending it when He tells them to move to the next place. This is your destiny—turn loss into gain for His glory. Wait, watch, and see what He turns your choices into.

CHAPTER 5

PTSD:
Put That Speculation Down

In this chapter you will hear the stories of how my children dealt with loss. Let me say this—they all had a different path to walk. They are living life successfully, helping others to grow through their experiences. Still reeling from the shock of Jack's death and having to plan a funeral that none of us wanted, my head was in such a fog that I paid very little attention to what my kids were feeling. When my California kids got home, they knew before they walked in the door that their father was dead. Even though I had spent the last 13 months caring for an invalid, I was not ready for their reactions. Without any notice, my youngest son fell into my arms as soon as he walked in the door. This woke me up and caused me to see each one of their individual pains. It has taken years to get us as a family to the place we are able to share with you our experience with loss, but I feel my kids have done an excellent job with putting their emotions on paper. Our hope is that if you are going through loss, their experience might also help you find your path through grief.

MICAH KLINE FROST: PROUD FIRSTBORN CHILD OF THE LATE JACK FROST

Being the oldest of my parents' children, I probably did not grieve the death of my father as hard as my other siblings, especially my sister. Also being the eldest came with good and bad perks. I had my dad a lot longer than they did, and parents usually are closer to their oldest child—sorry Sarah and Joshua. However, the oldest child is the guinea pig or trial experiment while a parent learns how to be the best parent ever or the worst one in history.

I probably judged my parents a lot harsher because of the negative things I experienced being raised by two generals in the Christian world who were trying to figure out life. But at the time of my rearing they weren't generals; they were simply Jack and Trisha Frost, my parents, who never knew as much as I did. By the way, my mom still doesn't, LOL.

When my dad was given three months to live, I was about to graduate college with my BA in business administration. I was planning to work for my parents in their business, but they soon closed it after my father's diagnosis. First loss—my job. I had just recently gotten married and my wife was expecting our son, Judah. Unsure about my future with my parents' other business, I decided to go to school to become a South Carolina state trooper. I was gone all week and only home on the weekends, so I did not really get to see my dad a lot in those last months before his passing. I came every chance I could to check on them, finally moving back in with them so they could have the help we could give them while working and going to school ourselves. My dad also felt that Majesta, being pregnant, should not be by herself during the last weeks of her pregnancy.

I am glad I had the distraction of going to school and learning a new job, because it helped me to cope with what was going on with my parents. I did not intentionally distance myself from them, but I am sure at the time it was not easy to watch my dad try and live life joyfully and be interested in our lives while enduring the high level of pain he was experiencing.

My mom has always had a strong constitution and was brought up with a hardworking ethic, never giving up and being faithful to the end. I watched her day after day carry my dad's fifty-pound oxygen tank up a flight of stairs so that he could sleep in his bed; I helped her carry him to the toilet until he was bedridden. It reminded me of how strong a woman she is.

Being the oldest child when tragedy strikes, you feel responsible to step in and fill the hole being left by the person leaving. I felt my duty as the oldest son was to look after my mom, but if you know Trisha Frost at all you know that she was not going to allow me to take much time away from my family responsibilities to help her.

My dad died right before I graduated from trooper school. He never got to see me not only fulfill a dream of mine but his also. He had, in the past, been a police cadet. My dad's absence from one of the accomplishments in my life did have an effect on me, but my mom was trying to exemplify the best she could that life has to continue.

My wife wanted to take our newborn son to meet her family in Florida. My mom felt there was nothing we could do to help Dad, so she blessed our trip. We had just arrived in Florida when we got the call that Dad only had a few more hours to live, so we cut our trip short and headed home. My dad died shortly after our arrival back home.

I know I cried as I watched my mom tell him goodbye, but again I immediately kicked into the duties of a firstborn child to step in and help my mom. I am a leader by nature, but my mom is also a strong leader. Yes, there is a lot of grief with the loss of a parent, but my mom and dad, through their example of living life in front of me, have taught me a lot about turning loss into gain.

No one wants to experience any type of loss, but when you do—and you will—what you choose to do after the loss will build your character. And from those choices, you can become more successful than your example. That is what happened to me. I chose to move forward into my career and to focus on having a new family more than I focused on the loss of a parent. My mom made a choice in front of us and the whole world to continue keeping the message of Father's love alive. I chose to support her decision and continued working for the ministry as their book-keeper while keeping my full-time job as a trooper.

There is nothing wrong with being a support structure instead of the leader in your family if that is what your parent needs.

I am often asked the question, "Well, how did you grieve, or did you grieve?" I am not one who shows a lot of emotion publicly, but yes, I did grieve and daily grieve over the loss of my dad in our family.

My dad will never be around to have our weekly breakfast. He basically would take each child out and just be available. I love my mom, but there is just something about a son losing his dad. You can't understand what it is to lose your mentor and your dad at the same time until they are not there. I can't run life decisions by him anymore; we can't go fishing or play golf anymore. At one point in my life, golf was the place that I could be alone with my dad and know he was for me. I will never get to see and hear my dad enjoying my children's successes in school and sports. In other words, that quirky big guy who is my dad will never get to experience those things with his grands, and I, his firstborn, will never get to see those quirky smiles from my best friend or hear those words: "You done good, son. I am proud of you."

I am very aware of the depth of this great loss, and in my own way I have grieved. My mom asked me to write my feelings and experience; I am not sure my path is the answer that will help you, but I know that in the midst of a tragic loss you must find your way to grieve the experience and don't allow others to tell you how. You get to make the choice when and how you need help to deal with loss. I have a great family around me; I have great friends who keep their eye on me, and when I have needed to deal with my experience, I do. So here is my advice for you—find your own path, but find it. Loss is hard, grief is harder, but you get to do it your way and that is OK.

SARAH FROST CREW: ONLY DAUGHTER OF THE LATE JACK FROST

My daughter Sarah and her husband Doug were probably the ones who were there for me the most. I don't want to measure loss by which one of my kids experienced it the deepest. There is no real measuring stick for the severity of loss, but if you judge it by emotions, one person's experience might seem greater than another's. Loss is loss, so break your measuring sticks now. I often think of Second Corinthians 12:9 when I think of how my daughter handled loss—in my weakness, His strength is manifest. The key here is humility. Sarah, a very strong person especially in how she wants to be perceived, had become very weakened with the losses she endured, so to be able to deal with her loss she had to come to terms with being weak at times so that she could allow Him to take back control of her emotions. She had to develop a trust in His ability to have her back. He chose her more for her weaknesses than her strengths because they amplify her need for Him. You are going to love her story because she is the epitome of real, raw emotional pain. Gotta love this girl—and I do.

There is probably no more terrible instant of enlightenment than the one in which you discover your father is a man—with human flesh.

—Frank Herbert

As I read this quote in my favorite book, *Dune,* that my dad had given me, I knew he was dead. I was right.

For the first almost-15 years of my life I wanted nothing to do with my dad. Then, in the space of about six months, he got hold of the message of the Father's love and changed so drastically that he became my hero. But the wounding of my early life left me with an extraordinary ability to not feel emotions. I remember one of the things my dad used to say that reinforced this ability in me: "You panic, you die."

I was about 19 when I began the journey of opening my heart to emotions as I was going through the School of Ministry in Toronto. I allowed myself to love my parents truly for the first time. So, when I lost my father at 25, my emotions went wild. I had never allowed myself to love anything enough to grieve or be sad over them leaving or dying. His death, and the utter abandonment that occurred after, left me in an emotional state of grief and shock that I had no idea what to do with. All these years later, some days I still do not.

The *very* basic story here is that 90 percent of the people we were in covenant with left my dad's funeral and did not call, check in, write, or pursue any contact with my brothers and me in any way. People whom we grew up with for 15 to 20 years walked out. Some kept up with my mom but not with me. I was a vital part of my parents' ministry for 10 years. I traveled with Dad and the team monthly all over the world. People I grew up with, vacationed with, ate dinner with multiple times a week were gone. Some were there for my mom—at first.

Doug and I were working at Bethel Church in California, but our cell phone numbers have not changed since I was 19 and this happened when I was 25.

Following the walk out, finances became super hard for us because we found out I was pregnant three weeks post-funeral, and I stayed home after giving birth. Daycare in California cost more than I made, so we increased in size but decreased in finances.

Doug handled Dad's death much better than I did. To be honest, I only know this because he told me. I was all about me during that season and did not even realize that Doug lost a father too. He finally had a dad after living most of his life with no dad, and then his new dad died and I went nuts. No one from home was there for Doug either. I went into severe postpartum depression. Our daughter was born with a sleep disorder that went undiagnosed for four years. We were trying to learn how to move forward through grief and depression while learning to parent at the same time. Our child, who was not able to sleep, cried and needed my attention every few hours. We were far away from friends and family who did not even check on us. It was our choice to live in California, but it would have been amazing if some of those covenant brothers of my dad had called us every so often for a season. We were depending on strangers in a strange land for help, with no sweet tea or grits. But the Lord did bring us a few friends who kept us mentally afloat. When we finally did move back east, I was too wounded and broken to move back to our hometown. So we moved three hours north to be near our friends—great people who helped me heal enough so that two years later I was capable of returning home.

I was still a broken, shattered mess going through another postpartum depression after our second child was born. Fortunately, God had placed friends around me, and they were brave enough to confront me and get me on depression medication. My relationship with God was still a hot mess. Sorry not sorry.

I didn't initially believe in physical healing. After a year of living in Bethel's environment, I believed maybe God might heal Dad and that He sent me to Bethel to learn this so Dad would be healed. So when Dad died after I had believed, I felt betrayed. I was filled with anger and bitterness. That is what loss does to an already wounded person. We allow the lies of the emotional reality to become our truth, at least for a season.

Guess what? Father can handle this type of season because even if you don't believe the truth and allow your circumstances to convince you of a lie, He is a pretty big guy and can handle that. My problem at that moment was being overcome with the loss of my dad. God was patient with me and waited for me as long as I needed, but I was too emotionally broken to be able to believe it.

God is OK with us feeling at times like He has betrayed us. What grieves the heart of God—and yes, God also grieves—is when we don't seek His hand for help. After all, God had the power. I felt He didn't use it the way I wanted to produce the outcome for us.

Most people will turn to God in times of loss with quite a different attitude than I had. I had questions that He was going to have to answer if He really was the Father He said He was. Why did He send me there? Why was my family abandoned in the middle of our worst crisis? For seven years I wallowed in anger and bitterness and hatred toward Him because I chose not to allow Him to show me my individual path of grief in the greatest loss that a child, even as an adult, could possibly experience.

Long story short, over the course of twelve years I came to two revelations. I hope it does not take you as long as it took me to get these revelations. I hope you learn at least one thing from my experience—God loves you just as much when you don't feel His presence as when you do. In your weakness His strength is manifested. Our best option is actually to humble ourselves and allow Him to show us His path. He knows the beginning from the end. I had heard that, but I could not trust that as long as I made Him perform for me instead of allowing myself to trust Him.

First Revelation

My dad always believed that he would be dead by forty—so much so that when he proposed to my mom he added, "If you can stand to be a widow early." Granted, he thought the sea would take him as it did all fishermen eventually. He left the sea and lived, but he was supposed to be in a wheelchair from arthritis by the time he was forty. But God issued a new decree as the king did in the story of Esther.

A man came to my dad and said, "You have got to change your diet and stop being so angry and aggressive. You have a call on your life and you need to be strong enough to carry it." So my dad changed immediately. He began juicing, fasting, and eating a vegetarian diet. He began to seek help for his emotional baggage. He healed himself and never needed the wheelchair. At the age of 46, six years after he thought he would be dead, he encountered the Father and took the message to the world. He died three months before his 54th birthday. During his short lifespan, he and my mom helped hundreds of thousands if not millions of people. John Arnott told my mom at the 25th celebration of our ministry to start saying millions because it was millions now.

Second Revelation

God sent me to Bethel not to earn Dad's healing but to protect me from Dad's brutal, tortuous, wasting away death. I do not remember my dad being sick because I barely saw him like that. I remember him well and healthy and thriving.

I had the first revelation within six months of Dad's death. It did not help, though. I was still angry and bitter for seven-plus years. I have spent the last six years working hard on repairing my relationship with the Lord. I still struggle often with Him. But I recently came into the second revelation and am processing and sorting through it. Life has been even harder the last six years than the first seven were. The physical, mental, and emotional torture of the last seven years has caused me to walk away from ministry altogether so I can focus on personal recovery. I heard once that if you don't take care of yourself, you won't be around to care for others. Doug is carrying on as the head leader of Shiloh Place now. But despite that, we have built a new family. And I am closer to God now, probably more than before Dad's death, even though I still wrestle with Him a lot. He is the first one I blame, but He doesn't mind my toddler tantrums. He takes them like a true Father and holds me anyway.

I am coming around thanks to His enormous patience and the patience and love of my family, specifically Doug and my mom and the rest of the family God placed around me. Things are hard during times of loss. Things are also not perfect. But my mindset is slowly changing and I am learning after almost 13 years how to maturely move forward with great loss and resistance. Even though I am not currently in ministry, I am currently friends with God. I'd rather that than anything else.

I told you that you were going to love her story because she brings a kind of rest and peace to those who have not found their specific path to healing. Thank you, Sarah.

JOSHUA FROST: YOUNGEST SON OF THE LATE JACK FROST

I was and still am my dad's biggest fan and favorite child, no matter what my siblings might say. My experience with this great loss and my pathway of healing from the grief entails probably much more than my other siblings because I am the youngest child. My brother Micah and sister Sarah would use the term "baby" here. I will admit that I am proud to be the baby and have milked it with my parents. That is a gain, but my loss, I feel, is greater because they got to have my dad longer than I did. My dad died when I was 21. The gain I experienced was that I had more time with the healed Jack Frost than the Captain Bligh Jack Frost whom they were raised by.

I was made in my dad's image and heart, but my personality is probably more like my mom's. So I am the best mix of the two of them. I love being light-hearted and a little quirky like my mom, but I also love my adventurous nature like my dad. Even when my dad died, I was experiencing the life everybody else wanted to live (for more details of that get my book *Sons of Destiny*). I was preparing myself to travel with my dad and be the lead speaker in their ministry. My dad was always a huge promoter of this message of Father's love, and because of that example I have become one of the nicest dads around. (I have four kids.)

I dealt with the loss of my dad, my best friend and greatest hero, by remembering the legacy that he was and left me to become. I am not trying to be him, but I am a chip off that block, which I am very proud of.

Most people with a nature like mine, the class clown, would deal with painful loss with a joke or being lighthearted. Maybe I would have too had I not been gone from home for several years. I left home right after high school at the young age of 17.

The best way to get vengeance on the enemy is to exemplify the example that you were given and become greater than it. At my dad's funeral closing I asked to say something. I told the guests there that even though we did not get the outcome we wanted, that did not mean that Father God did not hear and heal. My dad died of glandular cancer in his lungs. So I decided to grieve his loss my way and to trust in Father God to take vengeance on what killed my dad—cancer and lung problems. I asked anyone who wanted healing in their bodies of any kind of cancer or lung issue to meet me after the funeral and I would pray for them and believe Father would heal them. Only one person out of over 800 came forth, but today that lady stands healed of black lung that had almost shriveled up one of her lungs. That started my healing journey, but that was not even the biggest issue with loss that I had.

Years went by, and one day I realized that no one had stepped in to fill the void that my father left. I could have judged all of the revival people who talked about how much the Father loves you and how as a church we are family. No one, nada, not a person reached out to me to help with the things a father might teach his young son. Not one church member or father type ever asked to be there, or at least checked on me for a season after my dad died. For me this was another loss, maybe even as big of a loss as my dad. In my heart, even though I did not voice it much, they were liars and certainly did not live what they preached during the years my dad was serving in their ministries. This caused incredible disappointment in man because they say one thing and live another. But leaving home so early in life, I had already developed an independent heart that did not need anyone anyway.

I knew where my dad was, and I knew the message he left us to carry on was real and I needed help in finding my own path of sonship. A son needs a tangible example of a father, and at this point I did not feel I had one. If not careful with the rest of my life choices, I could have very easily become an orphan, so to speak, and be living my life from a mindset we call the orphan heart. (See my parents' book *From Spiritual Slavery to Sonship*.) So without a father figure in the church coming forth to be there for me, an almost greater loss occurred. I was losing my ability to believe that church was really a family.

My dad's friends, who had promised my dad that they would be there for his family, were not. None of the role models showed up at my wedding; they did not call or come when I had kids. To date none of my dad's covenant brothers have even picked up a phone to check on me at all. Yet they all made promises they would not forget me. One of my parents' old spiritual sons, Leif Hetland, is the only father figure (outside of my uncle and father-in-law) who has ever celebrated life with me and tried to offer me mentoring like a father would.

Being forgotten has the potential to make you believe the lie that you have no value. Another lie you might embrace is that fathers will abandon you. When you embrace those lies, you will eventually succumb to bitterness and rejection, which can turn into a critical nature within you. Had it not been for the message my parents carried and exemplified to me and the world, I too would have been the victim of those negative emotions.

My victory in loss was to grieve the pain by doing what my dad would have done, and that was pray for the sick or the lost, be there for others' pain and sorrow, celebrate life with my family and those around me, and keep my word and focus on courage and purpose. *When you focus on the pain, you lose hope for a good outcome, but when you deal with loss by grieving and forgiving anyone, including God, for being responsible for your loss, then you step into your destiny with a heart of courage.*

I like to see myself as the superhero Thor (I mean, I look like him so I might as well use him as an example). He was the god of thunder, in control of weather and the atmosphere. You are in control of the atmosphere around you. You can choose to allow rejection and abandonment a place in your heart that will eventually turn into bitterness, or you can do what I did in grieving loss. I decided to do what my dad would do. So I did. I prayed for healing and for the lost.

So I want to encourage you that no matter what your loss is, the only way to overcome it is to not give in to it. I am not saying not to acknowledge it—that would be a dumb thing to do—but I am saying as you acknowledge that you are in pain from loss and as you give up your right to know all the answers then you open up a door of faith that gives a clear pathway in dealing with the pain of loss. You have nothing else to lose, but everything to gain.

$\mathscr{P}$ART 2

Tales from the Crypt: Other Kinds of Loss

The word *crypt* can actually be another name for *chapel* or *church*. Loss does not always involve death of a person. Loss can be just as devastating when it is the loss of something we love, like a relationship or a job or a home. When the loss is through no or very little fault of our own, the trauma can actually be more devastating. In this section I want to introduce you to a few stories from a couple of close friends who have experienced such loss and how the church world responded to them. The catalyst that allowed them to live life was their ability to confront their disappointment in people they should have been able to trust and allow grief and forgiveness to work through their emotions. Their change helped motivate them to be the people of courage I know today. Pain is real in loss and grief, but covering it up and hiding from the pain will only stunt your maturity and destroy the plan for your life. Your success awaits you when you make choices of courage.

On a daily basis, I get to speak with people who have experienced loss in different ways than I have. Telling their stories in this book is a very high honor and I take the responsibility of telling them seriously. Why? Because our intent is to address loss without dishonoring those who were the source of the loss or gave really bad advice during the loss. Here are just a few stories of how loss can affect so many lives, but these few stories represent thousands more.

These are your stories too. Put yourself in their place and take advantage of their process of healing. They have overcome through their own personal choices to not get stuck in life. As we look at their losses and the way they chose to deal with them, hopefully it will give you enough courage to make choices to move forward out of pain into destiny the way they did.

When I interviewed these guys, I was amazed at all of their stories—especially the story of Char and Rod Reid and Libby Hathaway, because it is a different kind of loss. I was totally taken by their stories. They had the right to become bitter, angry, resentful, discouraged, and disappointed. They could have totally given up on believing that God had a plan for them. At times I am sure they probably wanted to, but they knew better than to sit in the pain of loss for very long. They knew their destiny was on the line in the choices presented to them during the pain they encountered.

Sometimes pain of loss can bring us into our next season of joy or happiness if we don't get mesmerized and lose focus. I am so very proud of these guys and the example they are to me and others of making courageous choices. I loved hearing their stories of choosing courage because they had no bitterness or negative emotions as they told me their stories. We cried together some, but not in an angry way. I think of the parable of the talents—when you are faithful with what you have been given, then you're given more. That is the outcome for these guys as they focused on the end result and the consequences of their choices.

CHAPTER 6

The Doorbell

The story of Glen, told by his parents
Nadine and Boodie Walters

The next two chapters are going to deal with a type of loss that I never want to imagine—the loss of a child. As we deal with the path of grief and loss in these two stories, we want to look at some responses from well-meaning people who should have known better. Why do we want to look at them? Because so many people have been wounded or abandoned by leaders who did not know how to deal with someone's loss, especially if they had no experience in the type of loss the person was dealing with. We are not trying to place blame here; we are trying to look at cause and effect in order to help heal you. We want to give examples of how to forgive those who might, however innocently, have added to the trauma that was already happening.

In this story you are going to read about trauma, not just of loss but when well-meaning people say things without thinking that have the potential to alter your life's course. Now, is it anybody's fault? Well, yes and no. When a person is trying to comfort someone, they need to make sure what they say is actually comforting and not just something they have been indoctrinated to speak, especially if they are leaders in a church. This next story might help you to find your pathway of forgiveness when well-meaning people say things that hurt almost as bad as the loss.

Everybody is always afraid of that "doorbell ring" that has the potential to be the bearer of bad news. Being the mother of a South Carolina state trooper, I dread it when someone rings my doorbell if I do not know they are coming over. So it was for Nadine. A neighbor rang her doorbell and gave her the news there was a bad wreck involving a car that looked like Glen's, her oldest son. Sure enough, it was Glen.

People on the field saw her coming and encircled around her so she could not see how bad the car was. Glen was still inside. On her way to the hospital, she felt this warm, honey-like feeling begin to pour over her—the Lord's way of comforting her and telling her that her son was gone. I believe with all my heart that Father never forsakes us in this fallen world where bad things happen to good people. He always sends comfort to us through the Holy Spirit.

In times of great devastation like this, we find things to cling to so that we can overcome the tragedy. I love how comforting the Word is during these times, but sometimes people need each other. Boodie and Nadine Walters were born saved, in my opinion. They are the epitome of kind and compassionate people. Not just because they are Christians, but because that is their nature and they are the first on the scene when tragedy or need strikes others. Having this nature caused them to turn to each other when tragedy struck their family. Statistics say that 16 percent of marriages that experience the loss of a child end in divorce. This may or may not be the case, but the loss of a child is a strain on any marriage.

People often blame themselves for being bad parents during loss. Glen did have some issues, but what child or what parent does not deal with issues when their kids are teenagers and early adults? When you lose a child to tragedy, grief is not the only thing you are going to deal with. Guilt comes knocking at your door almost immediately. All of a sudden, you are reminded of everything you should have done. That opens up doors in your heart to believe you parented wrong. Boodie and Nadine even heard that from some people. They were trying to offer help, but it was not the time to give their assessment and judgment of another's parenting.

Glen Walters grew up in a home with two of the kindest, most compassionate people I know. Since the first time I met the Walters at a community meeting in Georgetown where my husband and I were the Salvation Army officers, I knew that to be true about them. Our lives took different turns in the next few years, so I was not around when Nadine and Boodie lost their son, but I moved back during the time that they were mending.

Recently, I sat down with the two of them to discuss their loss and their pathway to healing from grief. They have always kept a united front and been there to comfort each other, but they both had very different paths for healing their emotional trauma. Let's start with Nadine.

I asked Nadine, "After the news of the tragedy, when you had had time to process life without Glenn, what did you struggle with the most?"

"The feelings of emptiness," she said, "knowing that I would never again get to live life with my son. I would never again get to hear his voice or experience his life. Would he marry or have children or what would he become in life? Those things were stolen from me."

For a time, Nadine gave in to the disappointment. When she tried to pray, she felt like her prayers were falling into an abyss of nothingness. She had fallen into what she now knows to be the dark night of the soul—a place where you don't feel. "I could not feel pain, I could not feel hope, I could not feel God's presence anywhere around me. I began to separate myself from others, so loneliness and hopelessness became my new friends. I had so many questions, but honestly could not ask any of them because at that moment I felt abandoned."

The good thing was that the experience of the dark night of the soul helped her to realize that there is no hope in life without finding His presence, so for a season Nadine simply had to trust that He was there even though at that moment she did not feel Him or sense Him the way she always had. She was numb. This was not the place she wanted to stay; she knew she needed to heal but honestly had no ability or energy to put into it. "Had it not been for my friends and family who basically carried me with their prayers and support for our physical needs, I might have become a statistic." It is very important to have that tribe around you, especially when you are facing severe loss like the loss of a child.

Nadine did try on her own to find her way back into a place of passion that she had known before and wanted again. During the "season of trying to fix it," she stumbled across a great truth that can help make your time in "numb-numbville" a little less. *When you have no energy to find Him, just show up and let Him find you.* She heard this at a conference through Shiloh Place Ministries. That one act of faith, letting Him find her, positioned Nadine for a greater awareness of His love without striving or performing. A place of no judgment for how you relate to His love—who knew it ever existed?

Nadine went on to say, "I freely gave of everything that I had, and I knew deep down inside of me that at some point I would give away my healing in this experience also, but that did not help me with feeling the pain of loss any less." The advice from well-meaning friends could not help either. Nadine was told by one of those friends that she, as a parent, was partially to blame for Glen's death and she needed to forgive herself. (This is one thing you never say to someone during their grief process. Your role is to help them heal, not condemn them for what you think.) Now Nadine had a new friend—*guilt*. She began to focus on all the "what if" junk. Do me a favor—stop that now. It will stunt you in any pathway to healing the grief in your heart.

There are times in life when our pain can be an amazing tool to use for others. It's called the wisdom of experience. Nadine would rather not have this tool in her experience box, but as long as she does, she might as well use it. That is one of the many characteristics of the Walters that I love. Two of the most generous people I have ever met, they give away more than they keep so that they get to enjoy watching others prosper.

I asked Nadine, "How on earth did you ever begin to even want to live again?"

"When a demand is placed on the Spirit of God within you to use your life's experiences so that others are offered hope, there is only one possible choice to make. You position yourself in His presence, and if He really is truthful about who He is, then He already knows the plan for the rest of your destiny. I will see Glen again, so in the meantime I will do whatever is needed to help someone who is drowning in disappointment in their sea of hopelessness because they have not found their pathway for grief."

Wow wow wow! Not me, Lord. I don't want that life experience, because I might not handle it as well as she did.

Boodie had a different response. He felt the loss, but being the kind, gentle giant that this man is, he decided if he focused on the loss he would lose his ability to be grateful for the time he did live life with Glen. So he decided to look around at everything he did have. He looked at his business and how they are so prosperous that they have so much to give away. He focused his life in that season by giving his full attention to the business. Maybe it helped him, but his relationship with Nadine and his other son David was hurt because he gave so little attention to them.

Boodie himself is the one who told me this. Like my son Micah, Boodie is not big on public displays of affection, but he loves hard. He is a quiet soul, but when he does speak it's like wisdom from heaven just landed in your heart. I love being around this gentle guy because he is one of those who shifts the atmosphere of the room as soon as he enters it. His quiet wisdom is deafening to those who are listening. Rather than tell people what to do, Boodie lives a compassionate and gentle life in front of people, but his inspiration is compelling. He will never tell you what to do, but if you need help in overcoming, he makes himself available to those who want to just walk with him. It might be in the woods hunting, it might be on his four-wheeler riding around his huge farm—wherever it is, you can bet on his stability to be found faithful during crises and to give away anything he has to those in need.

One of my favorite places to go is to the Walters' cabin. Last time I was there, I did this interview with them and cried at the honor to know this family who have walked their path of grief over the most tremendous loss a person could have. I visited for a few days, and during that time people came and went and

I was astounded at how they treated each person— their kids, grands, friends of grands, other family members, hired workers on a home project, and me. Each person was treated like they were and are the most important person there. So much of their path to healing was to do like my son and take vengeance upon the situation by being what Jesus was when He walked this earth—an example of the Father's love, generosity, and compassion.

For many who experience this kind of loss, if we are not very careful we will put our energies into whatever we can so we don't have to stop and think about the pain of the loss we have experienced. For Boodie, as a hunter, the perfect place to process alone was in the woods, away from civilization. Nadine also loved to hunt, but her gifting to the body was in the office of a counselor, so for a season she poured her time into loving others and helping them find their pathway to wholeness. But at some point, they knew that they would have to come together in their handling of loss so that they could minister together again. They did. Today they work alongside their church leadership team, doing the work of the ministry. They live the life of Jesus in front of people as they move forward into their destiny.

To sum up, their pathway through grief is very simple—be there, be available. You don't have to say a word; just show up. You will know how to handle great loss just by watching them and becoming the example that they are. Everybody needs a Boodie and Nadine in their lives.

CHAPTER 7

The Art of Forgiveness

Roger and Pat Gosnell's story of devastating loss

I tell everyone that they are my best or favorite friend because I am so grateful for them in my life. This couple, however, might trump most of the rest. They have been with me through great pain when I did not handle things wisely. They stayed in the relationship when I was not particularly interested in the advice they were trying to give, so they stood silently by and refused to leave me by myself while I was fighting to figure it all out. Everybody needs a Pat and Roger in their lives. If you don't have one, be one.

I admire this couple because, to me, maturity is in making choices to never give up, especially when your circumstances are as horrendous as what you are about to read. I don't understand how they chose the path of healing with the devastation and loss that they encountered, but I am so thankful for their example because it has caused me to want to stay alive in the midst of great loss and find my path of healing. *Why* and *how* are big questions, but the Gosnells' story might motivate you to start.

Pat was having severe headaches and had gone to the doctor. After all of the tests were done, a security guard came into the doctor's office and asked Pat and Roger to come with him. What the heck? Who has ever had a security officer come to your doctor's office?

It was the worst possible news a parent could get. Their son Tad was shot and killed on his job while closing up his store. Two young kids who had just watched a violent gang movie decided to act out a part of the movie. They wanted to know what it felt like to kill another human. Why Tad? Why did they pick his store when there were hundreds of convenient stores all around the city? Why his? Why him? Tad had a bright future. He was going to school there in Kinston, North Carolina and working part time to make extra money to live.

Can you imagine the questions that would flow through your mind? Instead of allowing those questions to flood their hearts, Pat and Roger fell on their knees and uttered loud groanings at the loss of their son, and then they prayed for the young men who killed him. No way would I respond like that! I bet most of you would not either. I would probably have left there in a rush and found a gun and a way into the police station, where one of the young men was being held, and that young man would have met Jesus that day. But Roger and Pat had a totally different reaction to their great loss. They knew they had to forgive in order to have peace for the future and move forward in their pathway on life. They understood what Bill Johnson said before they ever heard it: "In order to have peace that passes all understanding, you have to give up your right to understand."

That's not even the end of the story, but if it were it would already be a good one. What I think kept them alive during this season was continuing to pursue their relationship with God. Time passed and they headed to the Toronto Blessing revival. At the revival, they heard John Arnott teach on the topic of forgiveness. They purchased his book on the topic and Pat lived out that message for the next few months. I am not sure that it answered any of the "whys" for her, but it grew forgiveness for these young men in her and Roger's minds and hearts, even beyond their initial reaction when the news broke.

God always makes a plan, and honestly the pathway to that plan is clear. His word promises us in Matthew 11:30 that His yoke is easy and His burden is light. The meaning of *easy* in this passage is "well-fitting." We are the ones who muddy up the clarity when we focus more on the pain than the path to healing. Roger and Pat chose to focus on their pathway. Even though they had initially forgiven those young men, Pat still replayed it in her mind. I can't blame her. I would have lived out of that pain, planning the damnation of those men.

Roger felt he should go visit one of the young men, Tyrone, in prison. He called and somehow got an OK to visit him. This is a miracle in itself because a victim can never get into prison to see a perpetrator. We still do not know how that door opened, but Roger was quick to step through it before it closed. When one door opens a path of healing in your life, go. Don't hesitate—move. That same door might close too fast.

I can imagine that Tyrone might have been intimidated and playing over and over in his mind what he would say to the father of the son he killed for absolutely no reason. He might have been frightened that Roger would find a way to kill him in that meeting or have him killed in prison, but he allowed Roger to come. Take a moment and think about what you would have done in such a meeting with this kind of pain of loss. All I have to say is, "Incredible."

Roger took hold of Tyrone's hand and told him how much he forgave him and told him about the love of the Father. On the five-year anniversary of Tad being murdered by him, Tyrone gave his heart to Jesus while Roger was holding the very hand that pulled the trigger that murdered his son. Wow! I have heard this story many times over the course of our relationship and it never gets easy for me because I continue to feel the loss for them.

I am sure that from time to time they remember this loss, and even though it was 22 years ago, you never forget your child, you never stop longing to see them and hug them and express your love to them, and Tyrone took that away from them. How can you look right into the eyes of a murderer and not hate them for what they did? This is *The Importance of Forgiveness* (the name of John Arnott's book). This is the pathway of grief that Father had for Roger and Pat so that they could process the greatest loss they would ever experience—the ultimate sacrifice.

The Lord told Roger, while he was holding this young man's hand, that today the Lord was going to take the old Tyrone and turn him into a new creation. I might not have chosen that path, but they did. They forgave and released the memory of the pain to a Father who could relate to them. Another Father who had also given His Son so that others would become new creations. The path is to *overcome evil with good* because *love never fails*.

You might not be ready to deal with your loss on this level. We are not asking you to, but I am suggesting that you find your pathway of forgiving those who have hurt you so that you too can become the example of love that the world is looking for. As my son Joshua said, "I will take vengeance on the enemy by doing what he hates and that is loving what God loves and giving it to the world." Thank you to the Gosnells for demonstrating that kind of love during very traumatic loss. Now they give it away to the world. Do you see why they are my heroes and best buds?

I want to add this: when I can't forgive, I do what Jesus did. I go outside of myself to the greatest example of love and forgiveness—my Father. When Jesus could not forgive those who put Him on that cross, He cried out to His only source, the Father. So when you can't forgive yet or are not ready, just cry out to the Father, "You forgive them, Father, through me." *He will take that as your pathway and never abandon you on that journey.*

CHAPTER 8

Throwaways

Rod and Char Reid,
senior leaders at Victory Christian Fellowship

Libby Hathaway,
senior administrative assistant at Palmetto Preschool

I n the next couple of stories, I want to deal with the loss of relationships and how people in the church deal with people in the church.

ROD AND CHAR REID

Imagine coming home one day with the news that you no longer have a job. No one should have to do that, especially when you have seven children from the ages of five to sixteen. Rod and Char Reid had been invited to come and pastor an average-sized church in Georgetown, South Carolina. They started a building program because they knew the church was going to grow rapidly. They decided to embark on this new adventure in life with their tribe, excited about the potential to pastor people. They went ahead and invested in a new home as well. What happened next was unexpected and unexplainable, but it happened.

Out of nowhere, on the very day they were going to close on their new home, Rod was approached by his leadership about a new direction/vision for their church. In the middle of a new building campaign, Rod assumed it was about the new facility.

The new vision basically shattered what Rod and Char had envisioned for this season of life. The new vision was totally opposite of who Rod felt he was and where he, as the senior leader responsible to hear from God, was to direct this community of believers. Rod was not made aware of this new vision until that day.

Rod and Char always prayed to be passionate followers of Jesus no matter what was required from them. Be careful what you pray for and very specific when it comes to directional prayers! At the elders' meeting they were handed an answer to that prayer—one of the greatest opportunities of growth that a young couple could be presented with. They had a choice to make—become compliant with those in leadership trying to box them into a direction they were not comfortable with, or they could choose to obey what God had given them.

To do the latter, Rod would have to challenge those leaders to trust him in his vision for the future. He did, and they had to make the choice of their outcome. Rod and Char did not approach this with the intent of offering any sort of ultimatum when they shared Rod's feelings with the leadership. Since he was a young teenager, Rod saw what the plan of God was to be for his life.

For I am Wisdom, and I am shrewd and intelligent. I have at my disposal living-understanding to devise a plan for your life (Proverbs 8:12 TPT).

Having at my disposal "living-understanding" in the Greek means to *discover clever inventions*. Rod knew it was going to be very hard if not impossible for him to compromise his path. When you have a great relationship with God as Father, you will take every opportunity to find His plan. The leadership, however, felt differently, so they chose to go with what seemed to be the most popular trend in the church world during this time. Rod and Char could either be true to what they heard or they could cave and be put into a box/vision that was not their destiny. At this time, they had seven kids under the age of sixteen and a new house that was going to require a payment and now no job or ministry.

Challenging moments bring about the opportunities to grow by choosing to trust. They chose to move forward with courage and trust Father God. After all, they were people of faith. An acrostic by Phillip Brooks for *faith* is Forsaking All I Trust Him. Father God was about to challenge them in a different way. Rod says, "He challenged the brokenness of our lives to prove to us that we were children of faith and courage."

The board probably felt they had them between a rock and a hard place. They even suggested to Rod that he see a therapist so he could get in touch with his feminine side. The board felt that Rod was not in touch with his emotions because of his choices and response to life. They told him he needed to get in touch with his feminine nature.

During times like this, when we are presented with who others think we should be instead of the truth of who we are, issues in our life will surface. When people speak what they perceive to be a truth that you need to hear and you just want to chunk it, pause long enough to see if there is any truth in what they might be saying to you. Rod had given Father the right to speak to him through others, so he had to pause for a moment with this challenge to see if there was anything that he might not be aware of.

In Rod's case there was. Rod had some issues with women in authority (we call them "mother issues") that he had never dealt with. God would use this situation to challenge the brokenness of Rod's life and help him be able to see the issues of wounding in his own heart and change them. My husband Jack used to say that maybe you are only 2 percent at fault in a relational conflict, but you are 100 percent responsible to change that 2 percent.

At the time, however, Rod needed his authority figures, both male and female, to believe in him, to affirm him as God's choice for this church body. But they did not. The elders' board felt they could not trust Rod, when in reality they were failing to *control* him. So they attacked his nature and character. When someone can't control you, they begin to bully you by attacking your character. In the next meeting, they demanded Rod either change and go with their direction or they would no longer need his services.

Because of their experiences with God, Rod and Char could not see themselves strapped down to a seeker-sensitive church. They were a family of faith, and when you live a life of faith and trust in God there is always a well-defined relationship. Out of their own personal intimacy with a loving Father, they had to be that for others. But God was going to prove Himself not just as a Father but also as a nurturer by revealing His *mother heart*.

The mother heart of Father God is the part of the person of God that bonds with us. He loves us through the way He cares for us and our needs. He creates within us the ability to trust and bond in relationships. This was missing in some of Rod's relationships. It took a choice for the next season to unveil Rod and Char's life destiny.

You can't change the vision you have been given by God. If the plan of others is not God's plan, you must make the hard choice to obey God. I have always heard that you either have a vision, adopt a vision, or cause division. Rod and Char had to remove themselves from the box of wrong identity. Char told me that once they decided this was their path, they began to feel more comfortable in their own skin. They felt so safe knowing that through their obedience everything for their next season was going to be better than the last season. This is the epitome of courage, making them my new heroes.

They chose to abandon the security of the known for the insecurity of the unknown because they believed and trusted in God more than a man's word. This can be a very scary place if your relationship with the Father is not strong enough to bear the consequences of your choices. Let down by the board's decision to change the vision they had previously communicated, Rod and Char left gracefully. However, the pain of abandonment and loss, especially from those they trusted, could have stunted their growth forever and derailed their future—had they gotten stuck in a victim mentality. Yet instead of becoming victims, they ventured out into uncharted waters, trusting their future to an invisible God whom we call Father.

The weeks that followed were quite frightening for this family because they were in the sea of uncertainty. Rod began to believe the lie that he was possibly a failure because he could not provide for those seven beautiful kids and his wife during this season. A fear of failure, especially for the man of the home, can have devastating effects on any relationship, especially when you felt like you put your all into a plan and then it backfired. Rod faced disappointment, let down in what he had believed and now not knowing if his children would be fed. These moments of darkness present you with a false narrative about your capabilities. You are forced to find out what you honestly do believe. You will never know what you are full of until you are bumped. The Reids were challenged in areas that they thought they had faith in. Their faith did not prevent them from being fearful when confronted with their broken hope for a better future, the loss of their job, and their ministry.

The questions arise: "Father, did You not say...? God, am I missing You somehow? Maybe I did not hear Him correctly." Every disappointed believer, at some season in their life, questions God's plan for their future. When you are confronted with the choice to obey God or man, you might think the answer is a no-brainer—until you are there, faced with the question of whether you are really able to succeed. Don't put more faith in a man's assessment of you than in God's choice for you! The heroes in the Bible were chosen for their weaknesses much more than their strengths, and Rod and Char were not going to be an exception to this rule.

They knew they had to find God's plan. Not knowing what to do or where to go, they went to another man's church and submitted themselves to trust Father to show them answers. One by one, people removed themselves from the Reids' life. But one by one, new people began to surround them in this new life. Person after person came into their lives to encourage them. Jack and I were two of the people chosen to pray for their future and healing of the rejection from their church during this season. *Rejection from a spiritual family is as hard as rejection from our natural family.* For many of us, our church families are closer than our natural blood ones.

No one in Rod and Char's family was spared from this pain of rejection. Their children were too young to understand how their church family had pushed them away. Rod and Char put their kids and healing from pain as their first priority in life. God sent Rod other guys who began to take an interest in his life. They began to demonstrate the love of the Father and courage to this beautiful couple. That example of love caused Rod and Char to heal their family. (This part of the story makes me cry because it is a reminder of how healing came to my own family; see our CD on "Healing the Hearts of the Family.") Rod and Char took each child and individually repented to them for not being the best example of a father and mother and leaders in the church. One by one, each heart was healed.

Now, do they still today have to deal with that pain of being hurt by those who called them family? Yes. Next to blood family loss, church family loss is a pain that cuts deep into our emotions. At any moment, something can trigger your memory and bring up the opportunity to forgive again. Do you need forgiveness again for your judgment of the loss? No, but it does take time to rebuild trust when trust is violated.

There is more to the Reids' story of loss, but I will end it here with saying this: Loss is painful but can be healed. Today the Reid family is pastoring a successful and growing faith-based church built on relationships. They learned a lot of hard lessons on loss and found a healthy path to grieve those losses. They set the example of a healthy path to their children, who want to exemplify it to the world in their personalities. When you take life's lessons of loss and grief and you turn them around by listening to the plan of our Father, guess what? You can't accomplish anything but success.

Rod and Char have already identified those they call sons and daughters and they spend a lot of time walking with them, showing them how to love, how to provide conditions for development for those who call Victory Christian Fellowship their home. People who have been hurt and hidden are drawn to the vision that Father has for them. He will provide that platform for you just as he did for Rod and Char.

The path of grief for those who have been wounded by church family is to humble yourself before God and He will exalt you. He will cause you to succeed when you do this. The Word tells us that He draws near to the humbled heart. That is how and why Rod and Char are so successful. They are an example of how to turn pain and loss into gain and the fulfillment of destiny. I often say if their church were closer to me, that would be the church family that I would call home.

LIBBY HATHAWAY

Libby's story is a lot harder than most of the stories in this book or in the lives of those who have been challenged with disappointment and betrayal. Her courageous lifestyle is not known to many people— only the few she calls family and close friends. People never imagine that the ones they love will ever abandon them and disappoint them until one day there it is. She was smacked in the face with loss through betrayal and disappointment in her marriage. Yet I am so proud of this woman because of her heroic example of how she dealt with it. I would rather lose Jack to death than to experience the betrayal that Libby endured in her relationship with her husband. Had Jack done what I am fixing to share with you, he would have gone to heaven a lot sooner and I would be left with a prison ministry. Maybe that's selfish of me, but it's how I feel.

Libby's path could have been a lot different than it actually is today. She knew the consequences of unforgiveness. Those of you who know this woman and her story know that she was not perfect in her role in this, but she never said she was. Read her story here and be motivated by her daily choice to not become bitter, resentful, or lose hope that she would be cared for all the rest of her life. She could've given up on her purpose and identity if she had not forgiven. The ending was not the ending we would have hoped for, but we don't always get the outcome we pray for. You either choose to move forward, forgiving and letting go of the pain of your past, or you can stay stuck in the moment, the situation, and what was done to you. Libby, I am proud to say, did the former.

At the time of her loss, Libby was not perceived as the strongest individual you would ever meet. Maybe it was sheer stubbornness that made her choose not to pass down grief to the next generation. Today, she is so much stronger in herself and how she relates to others. Her testimony truly will motivate you not to lose sight of purpose even when you can't see the pathway clearly.

Libby was going to a weekend retreat at The Cove, the Billy Graham retreat center. Libby's husband, Floyd, had to back out of this retreat at the last minute, so Libby wanted to go on with her friends. Libby, the one person I could count on to think about me, called me with the last-minute invite. I had always wanted to go there, and this was the perfect opportunity because I would be with friends who constantly put me in the middle of things they did. This was a safety net for me. Wow, what a weekend we had!

On the way home, I dropped Libby off at her house. I did not go in but just jumped on the highway, heading home myself. I felt like I should have gone in with Libby, but I was too tired. I was emotionally exhausted, this being one of the first events I had gone to without Jack, and I just wanted to be by myself to process the happenings.

Just a few minutes later, the phone rang and Libby was screaming at the top of her lungs. All I could hear was that Floyd was "gone." I thought he had died. By the time I got there, her daughter had arrived and we learned that Floyd had left her. She and Floyd had had problems in their relationship in the past, but they always sought help and eventually worked most issues out, or so Libby thought. Then without warning, over the weekend he rented an apartment and furnished it with the help of some of his friends. Libby had no clue that this was the reason he had backed out of their weekend retreat.

Abandonment is one of the most devastating losses. It leaves the person being abandoned wondering why. What did they do? It condemns them to a feeling of uselessness because someone important has lost interest in them as a person without giving them an explanation. It sends the message that they are broken and have no value, and if they believe in that lie then they begin to live from a state of brokenness and they shut down. Their minds and bodies will actually respond to the message that they are broken in others' eyes.

At first, Libby did begin to believe the lie that she was broken and had no value because Floyd chose not to give her a reason; he used the excuse, "It's not you, it's all me." That is what a coward does. Now, maybe Floyd had a good reason; maybe their life together was horrible, but a coward takes the easy way out and it was easier to leave Libby than to confront the issues of his own heart. Feeling broken and abandoned, Libby could have given up on life. So many people do in this place, because the loss of a relationship through abandonment and rejection can be devastating. To some, it's more devastating than death.

Over the years since then, I have watched Libby make choices to replace the lie that she was "not worthy enough" any longer to be Floyd's wife with the courage it was going to take to protect her children and grandchildren. She did this by confronting the bitterness that might have begun to seep into her heart with the forgiveness that she had been taught and now had the opportunity to use.

Hebrews 13:5-6 says that He, Father God, would never "walk off" and leave her comfortless the way that Floyd had. In abandonment, the hardest choice is probably to really believe that word. It becomes a daily choice presented to the abandoned person to believe and actually be able to trust others not to walk away from you during this type of loss. Their expectation becomes, "If they left me, you might too." So it's hard to trust in new relationships. This person must make the choice not to believe that people will "walk off" and leave them. They must choose not to reject first, before they can be rejected and abandoned again.

Over the next ten years, Libby lost her relationship with her husband, his family, and the friends they had made together. Can you image what Christmas and the holidays look like for divorced people? Libby dreaded them, when in the past she had been one of those who got excited over them. She lost her church because Floyd was an elder there. The church never shamed her, but in her fear she expected them to, and she separated herself from any opportunity to feel shame. Many people tried to be nice to her the couple of times she did try to go back, but the questions from people who did not know the story were more than Libby could bear.

Libby never gave up hope that the relationship could be repaired, but the final end to their relationship came with Floyd's untimely and unexpected death. Floyd pulled out in front of an oversized pickup truck and was hit by the other driver, who never had time to brake. Floyd was killed instantly at the scene. He never had a chance to make amends with Libby and his family, even if he had wanted to.

At his memorial, there were many awkward moments because Floyd had another family during this time. He left behind not only his girls from his marriage to Libby, who are adults now, but a ten-year-old daughter whom he had while in a relationship with another woman. I watched Libby be a champion as her girls wanted her beside them so they could mourn while the other woman was actually in Libby's role.

When betrayal is involved, loss is very different. I know the pain of feeling abandoned by the death of my life partner, but I do not know the pain of that kind of loss with the betrayal of your life partner. Being betrayed can cause you to become suspicious of everybody. It is hard to start new relationships because you are tempted to judge another's motives. Without realizing it, you can develop an expectation that others will betray you also, so you create this wall of separation. Then, people who want to get to know you begin to reject you. It is like an invisible force field that you give off because the pain of the betrayal and loss has never actually been dealt with.

Libby decided early on to become aware of the emotions that she might not be dealing with so well.

She invited her best friends to speak to her when we saw her get bitter or play the victim card. (There are six of us and I am the favorite—honestly!) We refused to allow her to become a hermit because of her pain. Most of us actually wanted to send Floyd to heaven long before he went, but we knew the importance of helping her be emotionally free of trauma and rejection. So far, it is working for her. A real key to healing is to find that group of friends or family whom you can trust with your heart to say something when they feel you need help and hope.

With this type of loss, you may need to break a soul tie with the person who betrayed you. Break that tie with a simple prayer of forgiving the person who wounded you and releasing them from the pain that you have experienced from them; then send back to them that piece of them that lingers with you. The pain that you have experienced won't just vanish, but that memory will not be able to affect your heart and emotions from then on. The betrayal happened; don't try and deny it, especially not to protect someone who should not be protected—not even for the sake of children. That role belongs to the Lord, and He is perfectly capable of protecting your children.

The consequences of our choices are real. You have to let children learn from the examples of others.

Today, Libby has chosen her pathway through grief. She chose to not become bitter, which has made her better. She chose to stop believing in the lie that this betrayal meant she was broken and had no value without Floyd. She learned that she came into this world by herself and that she would leave this world by herself and that Father can heal any kind of loss, even if it shatters every hope and dream you have for a future. Libby now thrives in her own pathway of wholeness because she surrounded herself with those who value her. She takes the time to find her own purpose and destiny for the rest of her life. Pause, take a deep breath, and give your Creator the right to unveil what you are about for the rest of your life.

$\mathscr{P}$ART 3

Survive or Thrive: The Choice Is Yours

CHAPTER 9

A Place to Heal

I did not want this book to be a seven-step program for the healing of tragic loss. Nor did I want to remind you of the eight stages of grief. There are lots of other books on this. I wanted to make this a very intimate pathway of healing from tragedy and loss and tell you stories that hopefully motivated you toward your own unique pathway of dealing with loss, knowing it is OK not to respond the same way as someone else. I wanted to invoke courage and give you hope by telling you the stories of others who have experienced tragic loss before you and have championed an example of how to find a pathway of living life in spite of loss. Hopefully their testimony of their pathway of healing will motivate you to also overcome and live life again.

Your destiny awaits you; your identity is already in place. Healing choices are the only thing standing between you and living healed. It is time to start on your journey of valuing yourself again. I hope these stories motivate you and provide for you a courage to deal with the grief, the loss, and with those who wounded you, judged you, or tried to make you into their image for the rest of your life. My goal is healing, not blaming. Some stories might offend you, but just remember—life happened, we all have moved on, and I hope you do also. I know the other stories in this book, like mine, end with knowing that we are living life successfully because we are focused on the path and not the pain. They embraced the courage to forgive whoever or whatever so that they live their best life no matter what.

As you know, this is the hardest journey that anyone embarks on, but when you are comfortless, find comfort; when you experience loss and need a season of healing, don't be afraid to find what works for you. Each person on this earth is so different; not one of us has the same DNA or fingerprints. This is why it is so very important to embrace your individual, unique nature and not be defined by others. I do want to encourage you to honor even the ones who are giving you bad advice. You don't have to take their advice, but remember who they might have been in earlier seasons of life—people who did impact you at one time. They showed up and tried to love you out of how they have been loved. Right or wrong is not the issue. Be grateful for who they were to you during their season in your life, but move on, move forward.

So now, let's look at things not to say to someone who has just experienced a terrible loss and is grieving. We also want to look at some of the ways God might use you or something you can provide for another's comfort while they are processing. I read once that a smart person knows what to say and a wise person knows whether to say it or when to say it. I have been both, but now, hopefully, my story is the wiser one.

WORDS TO NEVER SAY IN A SEASON OF GRIEF

1. God needed the person in heaven more than you need him on this earth.

2. Maybe you should've prayed more.

3. Death is one of the seven forms of healing.

4. Get over it—we all die or lose things in life.

5. The devil killed/took them.

6. God killed them—it must have been His will.

7. It was not God's will for the person to live.

These words can actually cause more damage than encouragement. When someone is experiencing loss and trying to grieve, we can help more by just making ourselves available. Remember the old song "Silence Is Golden"? Sometimes it really is, but being silent doesn't mean you are absent. Sit in silence and hold them or just be there to provide comfort or meet a physical need.

When Jack died, the phone calls from around the world began to come. I am so very grateful for the world's thoughtfulness, but I could not keep rehashing how and why and what was going on now and what was going to happen moving forward with plans for his funeral. My friends Moe and Melissa Wells came up to me, took my phone, and asked me for a list of people I wanted to speak with if they called. They took it upon themselves to meet a huge physical need that would have emotionally drained me, leaving me with no energy for my kids or plans. Melissa knew I loved those little chocolate covered donuts, so she sent Moe to the store to buy me a big bag because I was not eating or drinking. During the wake, my "B Six" ladies with whom I live life and have fun also made sure I kept drinking as people stood in line to offer their condolences. Thank you, ladies!

Look for the things that help during crisis and loss and do them. I had to be reminded to eat and drink. I needed someone to take it upon themselves to get me food and water. Why do I remember that more than almost anything else? Because during a dramatic crisis in one's life, what others do has more value than what they say. Meeting physical needs, especially those they might forget, during a person's loss creates that environment of safety that a person needs. Other things you might do to alleviate stress for them during this time are:

- Buy food, not flowers—look for ways to meet physical needs.

- Wash dishes, clean their house, take their kids if they are young, bring meals or gift cards for meals.

- Just show up.

- Don't forget them or leave them out of things, especially if they have been to other things with you as a couple.

- Communicate regularly with them.

- Find ways to exhort them.

If we believe that God is omnipresent then we also have to believe that He cares about the smallest detail of our lives. James 5:11 assures us that He does. Even if you are reading this as a pre-Christian, there are principles and laws that work during hard times in our lives. Law is still law, like the law of sowing and reaping. I have sown a lot of comfort into others during times of loss. Just showing up to help alleviate loneliness is all a person might need at times. I have these friends, Roger and Shirley Coons, who call me up last minute sometimes and tell me they are coming to visit. I am a busy person and can't always be there for their visits, but most of the time I am. Why? Because those tell me that they never forget me, and they bring joy to my day because it feels like what our family did growing up. You just visit! When visiting someone, it says a lot to them. It says that you are making yourself available to them, no strings attached, no motive. This is how trust is established. Roger and Shirley are two of the first people I would call to be with if I was struggling with loneliness.

In helping to meet a need for others, you will reap people being there for you. That might seem selfish, but to me it is obedience to what Father is showing you for your day. I could write a whole book on this topic.

I'm with people all the time, so how can I still feel lonely at times? Most of the time when I am with people I am giving out. Even though I love being the one providing the hospitality, it can still be very draining. *We all need someone or something that gives life back to us.* I am not going to tell you what that should be for you. Knowing who you are in times of loss and what you need might be one of the most difficult things for you to figure out. For me personally, I need people in my life. But I also acknowledge now that I can be overwhelmed at times when I spend too much time with people. When this happens, I need to be OK with coming away and having my own needs met. So I started praying for someone or something that would give me life. Father addressed this in my life so that I would not be tempted to alienate myself from people.

Not too long ago, I lost all three of my pets within a couple of months—my dog Goliath who made me smile with his goofy antics, my dog Apollo who was lazy but was a gentle soul and offered love, and then my cat Shiloh who was a rescue cat. They all died in one year, so my house seemed really empty without a pet. People were over all of the time, yet I would still have bouts of loneliness. I live in a nice home with a pool, adult/child swing set, and a trampoline in my backyard, so I use my home for my family first, but I also use it as a place for leaders and pastors and their families to come for a rest. Everybody loves my "Tiki Hut"—my name for my home. But when I have too much company or people over, I have to come away by myself to recharge. Unfortunately, I still hate being alone in those moments.

My daughter noticed my grief with the loss of all my animals and suggested that I volunteer at the local animal shelter to wash puppies. I decided to try that—I didn't have to commit to care for another pet, but I could still enjoy animals. The first time at the shelter, I have to admit, was a very emotional experience. So many animals looking at you, longing to have a place in your heart. I could have taken them all home. The experience filled my need to be with animals while not having to be responsible for them.

I wasn't really looking for a dog myself; I just wanted to fill their need for human touch. Each time I would go and get a new puppy to wash, I would have to pass by this beautiful animal that sat in a ball in her bed and did not want to be touched. Capri was a mix of an Australian Shepherd and Lab. Just a few weeks prior, the shelter had delivered a litter of her pups. Her pups were taken from her as soon as they weened and she was the loneliest thing I have ever seen, always on guard with her ears up and her eyes cracked open. She was in the middle of postpartum depression, living her life alone in a cold pen with only a bed and a blanket. She would not walk or leave her bed unless carried.

I ask the handler what her story was. She had been beaten by her owners and was kicked out once they discovered she was pregnant and lived life in the wild until she was picked up by Animal Control. Her teeth in the front were broken where she was kicked in the mouth. No wonder she was and is cautious with a human's presence, especially a man. From the first time I saw her, I could not get the image of her out of my head. When I went back to wash more puppies, I would sit in her cage and just read to her. Eventually, she began to let me touch her but growled the whole time. I would take her outside and just sit with her because she was determined not to walk, so we did it her way so she could be at ease while she learned to trust again. There are times in life when Father has no problem with doing things your way until you can heal enough to trust Him and be able to hear who He has created you to become.

Eventually, I decided to take her home and foster her, hoping that someone would find her and take her. She got out and ran away the second day I had her. We hunted for five hours before giving up. I stopped and prayed to find her with the volunteer from Kind Keepers who brought her to me. While getting into our cars to leave, we saw her head pop up in this huge field by my house. We trapped her in the woods and I brought her back to my house.

It took Capri months to choose to trust those who surrounded her to love her. It took her months of me and my family just sitting with her beside her bed while she growled at us but wanted so badly to be loved and touched without being beaten. For some of you, you need that tribe we spoke about to show up and just be in your presence until you can learn to trust again. Today, six months and lots of patience later, Capri is a lively little girl who runs like crazy in my one-acre lot, chases a ball and frisbee and brings it back to you, and allows you to touch her as long as you are not a big man who overpowers her.

She is loving life again because she is learning how to trust in people who refuse to give up on her. Those sorts of people are there for you also. You may have to pray that you will be able to see and recognize them, but as you do they will all of a sudden just show up. I know when I first met Capri it was a divine appointment. Finding her again after she ran away was a miracle. In your life as you stay in your journey, you might be both. You might be that frightened little pup who can't trust humans—it is OK to be that for a season. Just like Capri, as you began to build trust again, ever so slowly, your life will heal and your plan and purpose will be revealed. Capri was exactly what I needed to fill a void in my life so that I won't be lonely because she gives me unconditional love. She really wants nothing from me but love. She makes me laugh really hard at her quirky personality. Her name given to her at the shelter was Capri, which means whimsical and playful. You would never know that from meeting her the first time. She has gone from being afraid to live life to knowing that she belongs and will never have to fear another human.

The reason I am telling you about Capri is there are seasons of loss that interrupt God's plan for your life. The choices we make during those seasons can alter our destiny if we don't focus on where we are heading in life. If you have been hurt or wounded by someone who should have been a part of your journey, don't get upset and focus on who or what was not there, but remember these scriptures:

> For He Himself has said, "I will never desert you, nor will I ever abandon you" (Hebrews 13:5 NASB).

> Be silent, all mankind, before the Lord; for He has roused Himself from His holy dwelling (Zechariah 2:13 NASB).

> "For I know the plans that I have for you," declares the Lord, "plans for prosperity and not for disaster,

to give you a future and a hope" (Jeremiah 29:11
NASB).

That means He's got this if you will make efforts to
find and choose His path for you. He knows the plan,
so why are we trying to alter it?

God cares, cares right down to the last detail
(James 5:11).

It is not good for man to be alone. I am so glad that
Father Himself knew that as humans we are going to
need more than our knowledge of Him as God and
Father. We need more than just an intimate relationship of knowing who He is; we need to feel Him.
We need tangible things from someone with skin on
them. We need a SLAP for our emotional needs—
Security, Love, Affirmation, and Purpose. Go slap
someone!

Jack was gone and I was given the mandate to carry
on the message. Others thought I needed to remarry
and find another relationship, and many tried to set
me up, but I knew early on in this phase of life that
this was not the plan for me. But I also knew I needed

an outlet for physical touch. I need life around me, and just having people over a lot was not enough. So I met Capri, a wounded animal that I can give love to and receive love from. She was God's path for me to meet my needs.

I hope the stories those in this book motivate you to hear from God and allow Him to meet your need during seasons of loss and grief. I believe with all my heart that Father brought my answers to me in such unconventional ways. I am so quirky and weird, and His answer for me had to fit me and it has and does. Pay attention to His answer without shutting it out simply because it may not come in the manner that you think it should. Be open to a different look at His provision. He will confirm it to you because it will fit you.

Take My yoke upon you and learn from Me, for I am gentle and humble in heart, and you will find rest for your souls. For My yoke is comfortable, and My burden is light (Matthew 11:29-30 NASB).

"For My yoke is comfortable" actually means it is "well-fitting." He has a path for you, a plan that is well-fitting for you. You will experience pain, you will experience loss, so when you do remember our stories and our journey and let that motivate you to find your intimate path as you sojourn with Him.

That's a Wrap

It has literally taken me years to write this story of overcoming loss by finding my pathway through grief and dealing with sorrow. In sharing my adventure in this, I did not want to give you a certain path because my path is mine. I chose to write what I wrote because there are so many different streets to travel on; they all have different names, but they will all end at the same destination—your destiny.

I have traveled around 700,000 road miles to thousands of different places all over the USA and Canada since Jack's death. I've learned this one thing—the further away I am headed, the longer it takes to get there. That is a real revelation, huh? It is really just plain common sense. You won't get there in a day if you are going from South Carolina to California, but if you stay on the right road (the process) you do eventually arrive. I know—I have made that trip about ten times now.

You might make some wrong turns; you might have to take some detours on your way—that is OK too. My friend Crystal Grainger who has traveled with me a lot says, "If you make a wrong turn on your trip, instead of getting angry or frustrated remember—you are fixing to see something that you might not have seen before. Pay attention to it, because all of our steps are directed by the Lord." I wanted to slap her and kiss her at the same time.

But that is actually some of the best advice I have ever been given because today I am enjoying my journey even when I feel like I have made a wrong turn in my path. So I want to encourage you with a few scriptures that keep me focused. I have to renew my mind, because if I lose sight of where I am headed then that is when the enemy brings lies, doubt, and fear. I can't allow that anymore in my journey. These are some promises that I cling to when I am unsure about how to move.

Do not yield to fear, for I am always near. Never turn your gaze [your intense focus] from me, for

I am your faithful God. I will infuse you with my strength and help you in every situation. I will hold you firmly with my victorious right hand (Isaiah 41:10 TPT).

I never realized that at such a young age I would become a widow facing loss, grief, and such deep sorrow, but here I am and there I was. I needed to believe in something that meant I still had value. I am thriving in life by remembering the promises that I have been given over the years, studying the Word, and positioning myself to believe and trust in them.

Jack did die; I did and have suffered loss. Good has come out of horrible situations for me and the authors of the stories in this book. Even though there has been no five-step plan, I hope that our stories of the goodness of God will actually help you to focus on the end result in your story. We pray that your story will end like ours.

Trust in the Lord completely, and do not rely on your own opinions. With all your heart rely on him to guide you, and he will lead you in every decision you make. Become intimate with him in whatever you do, and he will lead you wherever you go (Proverbs 3:5-6 TPT).

When you can actually let go of all the disappointments and seek His face for you in your personal story, then your answers will be revealed to you. I forgive the people in my life and the lives of my kids who hurt me/us. I forgive those other people who tried to tell us who we were without actually knowing us. I forgive those who abandoned us, those who actually wanted me to go away. I release them from any responsibility to be there for this part of my life.

Good did come out of a horrible season. We used our pain to bring us into an awareness of victory in the midst of feeling defeated. Don't allow your circumstance to cause you to believe a lie; it will dominate your soul and alter your course of destiny. I chose to walk through a horrible experience choosing courage so that I would not allow fear to overpower me.

My life is so full of joy and excitement now, especially around the holidays. Facing my unexplainable fear by bringing it out of the hiddenness of my soul caused me to want to live again. You will have to, at some point, deal with scenarios that seem like the greatest fears of your life, but my hope is to help you not just displace that fear but to embrace it and deal with it so that you will be free of any expectations that have become problems in your future. As long as you hide your fears, they find a place to operate in you, but when you bring them out into openness and find the courage to let Him find you, that is when you are delivered from dread and believing a lie that has torment attached to it.

I hope our stories in this book never become your stories, but if they do or if someone you know has one of these stories, I hope that our ways of dealing with the loss and grief empower you to find the same courage we did to find your way back home into His presence.

Today as I am tying up this book, I had the worst day ever with really trusting God as Father and healer. I read a story that was sent to me by a friend of one of the photographers in the movie *Unbroken*, so I am pretty sure it is a good source of truth. While making the movie *Unbroken*, one scene had to be shot on a certain day; no other alternative day would work for whatever reason. Well, it rained outside, and the rain could have ruined the scene had it not been for Angelina Jolie.

She made a decision to act upon the faith of the guy the movie was about. She humbled herself and bent down on her knees and prayed and asked the God of this man to help them. The rain stopped and stayed stopped until the final call: "It's a wrap."

Such a great story, right? But then I began to ponder: "I have been faithful to You, God, during the greatest crisis of my life, and I want my prayers answered like this." When I pray, I need immediate results. "If You can do it for a heathen like her, why would You not answer my prayers for the success of my life and family and our ministry?" Sound familiar to you Christians who might be reading this? Yes, another form of the prodigal son. By the time that you get to this point, you might be asking yourself this too. The story of the prodigal son can be your story. Let love find you. Remember, that story was actually a story about a prodigal father—*prodigal* meaning "extravagant." I promise you that if you lean not on your understanding but find ways to acknowledge Him, your ending will be just as good. No matter how long it takes (12 years for my daughter), He will find you as you ask Him to show you how to heal and who to allow into your process.

It is OK to experience anger, loneliness, and hopelessness during your process. I did, and as you read the stories of others, they did also. But in each story, they had the courage to trust, and you might have to make that choice also.

In seasons of loss a person will either shut down and maybe blame others or seek help. I hear people say all the time, "When God shows up, this and that will be taken care of." Yesterday something happened in my spirit. I don't know if something broke or what, but I have stepped into an area of trust knowing that there is no such thing as "when God shows up." I am choosing to acknowledge that His presence is there all the time, even when I don't see or feel it. I thought I was doing that already, but now I know I am. He has already shown up. The dilemma now is going to be whether I will acknowledge His presence and give Him control to do anything and everything His way. I will, I do, and I encourage you to position yourself to believe this also.

Your life in the future, your destiny, depends on the choices you make during any season of loss. The sooner you realize this and change your focus to Him, the less time it will take for you to heal. I guess I lived with the new Jack too long to focus on anything else but destiny. My identity never changed; what changed was my desire to live from the healing that my husband chose—a healing that now has touched more than a million lives. (That is not pride—that is destiny fulfilled!)

Your destiny is your choice, but your identity was Father God's choice for you. Years ago, before the revelation of how much I am loved by God, I might have made a different choice. He proved to me how much He cares; now I cannot make a choice to have my outcome be anything but a testimony to the goodness of God and to the great love of my Father.

Don't be fooled and allow your circumstance to lie to you. Remember, you are in a fight for your soul. The outcome, should you choose it, is *you win*. But He loves you the same no matter what choice you make. You can end as a victim or you can end as a conqueror. I chose to stay in the race as a conqueror and take as many hurt people with me in pursuit of what Father intends for our lives. My prayer for you as you read this is *focus on what He is focused on!* His love for you. I did, I have, and I am finishing well.

If you need further help, check out more of our resources at www.shilohplace.org. If you get stuck, those books will help you. If you need help to identify lies in your life, our book *Unbound: Breaking Free of Life's Entanglements* could help you with that. I live today for the testimonies of courage in other people's stories. I had a lady from Germany contact me at 5:00 this morning and tell me how our books had changed her life and how much revelation was applicable to her situation. She thanked me for being a catalyst to her healing journey. Yesterday, I got to speak at the billionaire businessmen's Bible study, and they are going through our book *Experiencing the Father's Embrace* as a Bible study to motivate them to love their families first then take it into the business arena.

You see, this is why I stay in the race. Not for money (but provision is nice), not for success (that comes automatically for me), but for this "one more." The one more might be you, and we might not ever meet, but you are worth the journey—a choice I make today to stay in the process. There is always more revelation to be applied, but you have all of the love right now that you are ever going to get. The problem might be you allow your pain to dictate your future instead of focusing on the love He always has had for you.

When my circumstance tries to tell me about my God, I stop in the moment and recognize the lie and make a choice to find the truth. A big help for me was believing the truth of what those who know me now say. John and Carol Arnott, the founders of the Toronto Blessing, called me a champion; Bill and Beni Johnson, motivational speakers, authors, and the senior leaders at Bethel Church in Redding, California say I am one of the most transparent and courageous people they have ever known; Leif Hetland, another well-known author and president of Global Missions Awareness, says, "Trisha is a dream releaser who will cause eagle Christians to soar higher." There is so much more being said about me that helps me "keep the momentum of a life-changing message alive" (Paul and Sue Manwaring). That is my path and according to spiritual generals like the ones above I must be doing/living it well.

The last thing I want to say is that not only is it important to renew your mind so you know who you are, but also remember Father God knows too. He does not like it when those who are against you try to detour your journey. The only way to stop that is to know what He says about you. A part of my healing journey is to help others find their identity in who He says they are too and to help them live out their destiny through helping them commit to their path of healing that will lead them back to knowing that the *adventure in the venture* will always be exciting, hopeful, and, yes, filled with danger and risk. I think all of us want our journeys to have some excitement in them. I will leave you with some of my favorite scriptures that help me to remember who He is and always has been in my life.

Many, O Lord my God, are Your wonderful works which You have done; and Your thoughts toward us cannot be recounted to You in order; if I would declare and speak of them, they are more than can be numbered (Psalm 40:5 NKJV).

Do you realize that there are not enough numbers to count the thoughts that He has for me and you?

My beloved friends, let us continue to love each other since love comes from God. Everyone who loves is born of God and experiences a relation-ship with God. The person who refuses to love doesn't know the first thing about God, because **God is love**—*so you can't know him if you don't love. This is how God showed his love for us: God sent his only Son into the world so we might live through him. This is the kind of love we are talking about—not that we once upon a time loved God, but that he loved us and sent his Son as a sacrifice to clear away our sins and the damage they've done to our relationship with God* (1 John 4:8-10).

If I give everything I own to the poor and even go to the stake to be burned as a martyr, but I don't love, I've gotten nowhere. So, no matter what I say, what I believe, and what I do, I'm bankrupt without love. Love never gives up. Love cares more for others than for self. Love doesn't want what it doesn't have. Love doesn't strut, doesn't have a swelled head, doesn't force itself on others, isn't always "me first," doesn't fly off the handle, doesn't keep score of the sins of others, doesn't revel when others grovel, takes pleasure in the flowering of truth, puts up with anything, trusts God always,

*always looks for the best, never looks back, but
keeps going to the end* (1 Corinthians 13:4-7).

If God is love and His thoughts toward us are more
than can be counted by numbers, and if His love can
think no evil, then my question to you is: why are you
embracing a lie when you try and decide what He is
thinking? I had to come to terms with that as I made
choices to move forward into my life after Jack and
the many losses I have had since and because of his
death. You can too. You can choose life or you can
choose death. It's all focused on your ability to make
choices to trust in the one who gave you life.

The wonderful stories of the people who refused
to allow the pain of loss to dictate their destiny are
some of the most courageous lives I know. Their stories are your stories too. I thank each one of them
for allowing me to share their painful stories of loss
and how they made choices in the midst of pain to
believe that they belong and are loved even in loss. I
hope our stories of courage in the midst of pain will
motivate you to live life again. If this motivates even
one person, remember this: God your Father put you

into our path to encourage you to choose His life of courage.

Remember—acknowledge the pain of the loss, acknowledge your emotions in the loss.

Acknowledge any fear of moving forward into healing. If it doesn't feel safe, find a place or person you feel safe enough with to find your own path so that you will be the strongest you can be. In the words of one of the wisest doctors of our time, Dr. Seuss: *"Today you are you, that is truer than true. There is no one alive who is youer than you."* Trust in the one who knows you best. If you are a pre-Christian, all of the wisdom I have learned can still help you. Humility and being able to forgive those who have wounded you are your first steps too. That does not mean you actually have to forgive in your own strength; sometimes we just need to acknowledge that we need help in doing this.

Remember this: you don't have to be alone in your process unless you choose to be. He never forgets me in my process; He has a better plan if I will submit to it.

Furthermore, we had earthly fathers to discipline us, and we respected them; shall we not much more be subject to the Father of spirits, and live? (Hebrews 12:9 NASB)

Submit to the mission of the Father and live. He cares right down to the last detail and will actually show you His plan and allow you to make the choice if you are ready to trust it.

We count those blessed who endured. You have heard of the endurance of Job and have seen the outcome of the Lord's dealings, that the Lord is full of compassion and is merciful (James 5:11 NASB).

Life is not this way forever. Enjoy each moment, make each person feel they have value, remember those you have forgotten and love at all times. It has worked for me. This is my path; it does not have to be yours, but maybe something I have learned will motivate you to *stay in the process.*

That's a wrap!

About Trisha Frost

Jack and Trisha experienced many things through the 35 years of their relationship—some joyful and exciting, others disappointing and wounding. They lived, loved, and fought their way into finally finding their destiny. From their life journey to find the love they had so desperately been seeking came a revelation of unconditional agape love that brought healing to their family and also to the lives of many families around the world as they traveled and shared their story. Now the message of agape continues in the life of Trisha and their children.

Jack for years encouraged Trisha to tell her side of the story, saying to the Shiloh Place staff, "There is a Niagara Falls of teaching in her, waiting to be released," but until now the circumstances of life and ministry have kept her travel schedule at a minimum.

After Jack's death, Trisha began to travel, teaching her side of the story. Trisha was prophesied over after Jack's death that she was an identity crisis prevention manager, and she focuses her side of the story with that goal in mind—helping those who seek her out to find their destinies by revealing what hinders them.

As one of many Shiloh Place teachers, she, along with her team, has learned how to chart her way through new challenges of life without Jack. Trisha's life used to flow from feeling like an orphan, abandoned by her own loving father and then by her husband; she felt she constantly had to take a back seat to Jack's other loves. Now she can take you on the journey to find your place in the heart of a loving God as she shares the breakthrough of her own revelation of love and how she navigated through the grief and loss that has caused her to find and live her purpose.

Today, she lives her life foremost as a favored child of God, then as a mother to her adult children, helping them understand their own journeys of sorrow, loss, and grief. Trisha has also been told that Father is putting the *adventure* (thrill, elation, revival) back into her *venture* (proceeding in spite of possible risk or danger), and choosing this lifestyle has given her the courage she needed to live life continuing the message that Father is good, He keeps His word, and He never abandons you, especially through loss. Trisha lives in Little River, South Carolina and is Nana to nine beautiful grandchildren.

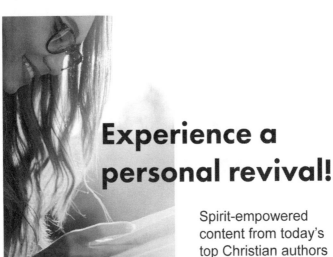